Human Rights Law
2012–2013

Routledge
Taylor & Francis Grou

LONDON AND NEW YOR

D1392698

1·48

Fourth edition published 2012
by Routledge
2 Park Square, Milton Park, Abingdon, Oxon OX14 4RN

Simultaneously published in the USA and Canada
by Routledge
711 Third Avenue, New York, NY 10017

Routledge is an imprint of the Taylor & Francis Group, an informa business

© 2012 Routledge

First edition published by Cavendish Publishing Limited 2003
Third edition published by Routledge 2010

British Library Cataloguing in Publication Data
A catalogue record for this book is available from the British Library

ISBN: 978-0-415-68340-1 (pbk)
ISBN: 978-0-203-30060-2 (ebk)

Typeset in Rotis
by RefineCatch Ltd, Bungay, Suffolk

Printed and bound in Great Britain by
TJ International Ltd, Padstow, Cornwall

Contents

Table of Cases

Table of Conventions and Statutes

European Convention on Human Rights – Articles and Key Cases at a Glance

Article 1 The Obligation to Respect Human Rights	NB This Article is not incorporated into the Human Rights Act 1998
The High Contracting Parties shall secure to everyone within their jurisdiction the rights and freedoms defined in Section I of this convention	
Article 2 Right To Life	Paton v UK [1981], Kelly v UK [1993], Jordan v UK [2001], Thompson and Venables v News Group Newpapers and Others [2001], Edwards v UK [2002], Pretty v UK [2002]
Article 3 Prohibition of Torture	Ireland v UK [1976], Askoy v Turkey [1996], Adin v Turkey [1997], Selmouni v France [2000], Napier v The Scottish Ministers [2001], Saadi v Italy [2008]
Article 4 Prohibition of Slavery and Forced Labour	Siliadin v France [2006], Van de Mussele v Belgium [1983]
Article 5 Right to Liberty and Security	Cabellero v UK [2000], Jordan v UK [2001], A and Others v UK [2004] NB note derogations under Art 15
Article 6 Right to a Fair Trial	Golder v UK [1975], Airey v Ireland [1979], Campell and Fell v UK [1984], Saunders v UK [1994], R v Twomey and others (No.2) [2011]

How to use this book

Welcome to this new edition of Routledge Human Rights Lawcards. In response to student feedback, we've added some new features to these new editions to give you all the support and preparation you need in order to face your law exams with confidence.

Inside this book you will find:

▨ NEW tables of cases and statutes for ease of reference

■ Revision Checklists

We've summarised the key topics you will need to know for your law exams
and broken them down into a handy revision checklist. Check them out at
the beginning of each chapter, then after you have the chapter down, revisit
the checklist and tick each topic off as you gain knowledge and confidence.

Sources of law

1

Primary legislation: Acts of Parliament	■
Secondary legislation	■
Case law	■
System of precedent	■
Common law	■
Equity	■
EU law	■
Human Rights Act 1998	■

▨ Key Cases

We've identified the key cases that are most likely to come up in exams. To help you to ensure that you can cite cases with ease, we've included a brief account of the case and judgment for a quick aide-memoire.

HENDY LENNOX v GRAHAME PUTTICK [1984]

Basic facts
Diesel engines were supplied, subject to a *Romalpa* clause, then fitted to generators. Each engine had a serial number. When the buyer became insolvent the seller sought to recover one engine. The Receiver argued that the process of fitting the engine to the generator passed property to the buyer. The court disagreed and allowed the seller to recover the still identifiable engine despite the fact that some hours of work would be required to disconnect it.

Relevance
If the property remains identifiable and is not irredeemably changed by the manufacturing process a *Romalpa* clause may be viable.

▨ Companion Website

At the end of each chapter you will be prompted to visit the Routledge Lawcards companion website where you can test your understanding online with specially prepared multiple-choice questions, as well as revise the key terms with our online glossary.

You should now be confident that you would be able to tick all of the boxes on the checklist at the beginning of this chapter. To check your knowledge of Sources of law why not visit the companion website and take the Multiple Choice Question test. Check your understanding of the terms and vocabulary used in this chapter with the flashcard glossary.

■ Exam Practice

Once you've acquired the basic knowledge, you'll want to put it to the test. The Routledge Questions and Answers provides examples of the kinds of questions that you will face in your exams, together with suggested answer plans and a fully worked model answer. We've included one example free at the end of this book to help you put your technique and understanding into practice.

QUESTION 1

What are the main sources of law today?

Answer plan

This is, apparently, a very straightforward question, but the temptation is to ignore the European Community (EU) as a source of law and to over-emphasise custom as a source. The following structure does not make these mistakes:

■ in the contemporary situation, it would not be improper to start with the EU as a source of UK law;

■ then attention should be moved on to domestic sources of law: statute and common law;

■ the increased use of delegated legislation should be emphasised;

■ custom should be referred to, but its extremely limited operation must be emphasised.

ANSWER

European law

Since the UK joined the European Economic Community (EEC), now the EU, it has progressively but effectively passed the power to create laws which are operative in this country to the wider European institutions. The UK is now subject to Community law, not just as a direct consequence of the various treaties of accession passed by the UK Parliament, but increasingly, it is subject to the secondary legislation generated by the various institutions of the EU.

The origins of human rights law

1

This chapter examines the emergence of human rights law in the domestic legal systems of the West in the 18th century and the later emergence of international human rights law in the 19th and 20th centuries.

THE EMERGENCE OF HUMAN RIGHTS LAW IN DOMESTIC LEGAL SYSTEMS IN THE WEST

In Britain, the Bill of Rights enacted in 1688 saw the end of the 'divine rule' of kings with power ceded to Parliament, and like the Magna Carta of the 13th century it is often regarded as a precursor of human rights law. In truth these texts are more settlements between powerful interest groups, and one must look further to the great texts of 100 years later – the Declaration of Independence and the Bill of Rights in America and the *Déclaration des droits de l'homme et du citoyen* in France – for what one may properly recognise as modern human rights law. These revolutionary documents rested on three principles:

1 *Universal inherence* – every human being has certain rights which are not conferred on him (or her) but which inhere in him by virtue of his humanity alone.
2 *Inalienability* – he cannot be deprived of those rights by another or by his own acts.
3 *The rule of law* – just laws must be applied consistently, independently, impartially and with just procedures.

To put these principles into practice, the US and France employed written constitutions to declare and entrench a catalogue of fundamental rights – a method subsequently adopted by virtually every other nation in the world. The traditional method adopted in Britain for protecting human rights in the absence of a written constitution and the resistance to entrenchment is examined in Chapter 3.

With the emergence of these principles, there remained the burning question among jurists of what source these principles and any consequent laws had for their legitimacy. Throughout the development of all legal systems, the difficulty has been in establishing a plausible source for a standard against which the legitimacy of laws may be judged. In the Middle Ages, claims for a 'divine' source of law revealed in Holy Scripture served to give legitimacy to State rulers.

However, as Paul Sieghart explains in his book, *The International Law of Human Rights* (1983), this 'single un-critical Christian based source of laws' was already being questioned during the 15th century renaissance, was fragmented by reformation in the 16th and 17th centuries and was eventually 'openly challenged by the Enlightenment in the eighteenth century and the rapid advances of natural science in the nineteenth'.

The resultant search for a new source of laws saw the development of the major political philosophies in the writings of those such as Locke, Montesquieu, Rousseau, Paine, Bentham and Marx. Some asserted the principles to be self-evident truths, others that they could be derived from the ancient theory of 'natural law'. Some argued that they derived authority from a 'social contract' between the ruler and his subjects, while others like Jeremy Bentham rejected such principles of law altogether as insufficiently specific. In his polemical attack *Anarchical Fallacies*, written in the 1790s in response to the declaration of rights issued in France, Bentham rejected any concept of 'natural rights' or laws existing above all others, famously describing the idea as 'nonsense upon stilts'. He believed that laws could only exist because government made them and could enforce them ('legal positivism'). While Bentham's philosophies were extremely influential in the adoption of much progressive social legislation in the UK, it is these same arguments against the concept of any fundamental or higher law that so greatly hindered the adoption of international human rights law. Many of his objections continue to be influential in contemporary political philosophy.

THE EMERGENCE OF INTERNATIONAL HUMAN RIGHTS LAW

The fundamental principle underlying the 'law of nations' is that of sovereignty. According to that principle, a sovereign state has complete freedom to deal with its own nationals and territory as it wishes. By seeking to impose restraints from outside, the development of international law runs contrary to the strict application of the principle. The adherence to this principle, combined with the rejection by the positivists, such as Bentham, of any inherent, inalienable fundamental laws, greatly slowed the adoption of international human rights law.

The 19th century saw the slow emergence of modern international law in the West. However, the pacts and agreements formed during that century did little to protect individual human rights directly and for the most part were concerned with ensuring stability and co-operation at State level. There were a number of enlightened international conventions such as those to abolish slavery; however, beyond those, the protection of individual rights by international convention was limited.

The horrors of the First World War awakened a new sense of purpose. In the peace treaties that ended the War, the League of Nations was established for the promotion of international peace and security, and the International Labour Organisation (ILO) was established for the protection of workers' rights. The League of Nations declared itself guarantor for the rights of ethnic minorities within the new State territories, a precursor of later human rights instruments. However, the League oversaw as many failures as it did successes. The continuing ascendance of positivist theories and the strict application of the doctrine of national sovereignty ultimately led to the rise of fascism and totalitarianism. The failure of the Disarmament Conference and Germany's withdrawal from the League in 1933 highlighted the League's impotence.

The League's chief success lay in providing the first pattern for a permanent international organisation, a pattern on which the later United Nations (UN) was modelled. The League's failures were due as much to the indifference of the great powers (which preferred to reserve decisions on important matters to themselves) as to weaknesses of the organisation.

AFTER THE SECOND WORLD WAR

The unprecedented atrocities that were carried out with complete legality under National Socialist legislation in Germany during the 1930s and 1940s, and similarly by the regime in the USSR, spelt the political end for both the strict theory of legal positivism and the strict application of the doctrine of national sovereignty. The Second World War would sweep aside any remaining reluctance about impinging on national sovereignty. It was now abundantly clear that the basic rights of individuals needed to be protected in international law.

When the War ended, and in an attempt to avoid such a cataclysm in the future, the victorious nations established the UN with a view to providing international safeguards in the relationship between governments and their own subjects. The UN had 50 members in 1945; it now has approaching 200 members.

Article 1 of the United Nations Charter of 1945 seeks among its purposes 'to achieve international co-operation ... in promoting and encouraging respect for human rights and for fundamental freedoms for all'. Articles 55 and 56 record the 'pledge' of UN Member States to take joint and separate action to achieve 'universal respect for, and observance of, human rights and fundamental freedoms for all'.

The UN's initial task after the War was to formulate an up-to-date catalogue of human rights and freedoms to be incorporated into international law. Drawing upon the many existing systems of domestic human rights law, the Universal Declaration of Human Rights (UDHR), the first international catalogue of human rights and fundamental freedoms, was adopted by the UN General Assembly in Paris in 1948.

The establishment of the UN, a 'global' organisation, was quickly followed by the establishment of regional organisations with similar aims adapted to the needs of more closely related groups of Member States (eg, the Organization of American States (1948) and the Council of Europe (1949)). Similarly, the UDHR inspired several regional conventions. Less than two years after the adoption of the UDHR, the west-European Member States of the Council of Europe drafted the European Convention on Human Rights (ECHR), which entered into force in 1953.

The ECHR provisions were in many aspects more detailed than those of the UDHR; clearly, agreement on more detailed provisions is easier and quicker to achieve among governments within the same geographic region, sharing a common history and cultural tradition. In general, regional treaties or conventions are apt to apply more stringent obligations upon their member states. However, the UDHR was eventually supplemented by two more detailed covenants: the International Covenant on Civil and Political Rights (ICCPR) and the International Covenant on Economic, Social and Cultural Rights (ICES). The ICCPR does provide greater protection than the ECHR in respect of certain rights, such as non-discrimination, a fair trial and treatment while in detention; also, the ECHR mainly confined itself to the protection of civil and political rights. Yet the diverse ideologies and traditions of the UN Member States delayed the Twin Covenants coming into force until 1976.

The crucial differences between the ECHR and the global covenants are the provisions for application and enforcement, which in the case of the regional

5

Development of international human rights law

National sovereignty

▽

19th century

1 International treaties included:
   1814: Congress of Vienna (after downfall of Napoleon I)
   1856: Declaration of Paris (international law of the sea)
   1909: Declaration of London (international code of
      maritime law)

2 During **1800s**, international doctrine of 'humanitarian
   intervention' developed in foreign policies of several
   European countries in response to state atrocities (eg those
   of the Ottoman Empire)

3 **1864: Geneva Convention** — humane treatment of
   wounded

4 **1899/1907: The Hague Conferences** — attempts to
   formulate certain rules of international law and
   establishment of **The Hague Tribunal**

First World War

1 **1919:** Versailles Treaty saw establishment of:
   League of Nations (for promotion of international peace
   and security and as guarantor of rights of minorities)
   International Labour Organization (ILO: to seek further
   social justice)

2 **1929: Geneva Convention** (relative to the treatment of
   prisoners of war)

3 Growth of international law hindered by ascendance of legal
   'positivism' (rejection of higher moral or 'natural' laws) and
   strict application of doctrine of national sovereignty.
   Ultimately led to National Socialist regime in Germany and
   historically unprecedented atrocities. Similarly, foreign
   criticism rejected as illegitimate by USSR regime

▽

Second World War

1 **1941:** 'United Nations' first coined by Roosevelt to describe countries fighting against Axis powers

2 **1942:** Declaration by these 'United Nations' pledging themselves to defend life, liberty, independence and religious freedom and to preserve human rights and justice

3 **1944: Dumbarton Oaks Conference** saw proposals for charter for a new organisation, the United Nations, to 'promote respect for human rights and fundamental freedoms'. **UN Charter** adds the phrase 'for all, without distinction as to race, sex, language or religion'

4 Establishment of new intergovernmental organisations specifically concerned with relations between governments and their own subjects:

Globally: **1945: United Nations**
Regionally: **1948: Organization of American States**
1949: Council of Europe

1948: Universal Declaration of Human Rights

1950 (in force 1953):
European Convention on Human Rights
1966 (in force 1976):
Twin UN Covenants
1969 (in force 1978):
The American Convention
1981 (in force 1986):
The African Charter

covenant go much further than the UN covenants. The ECHR established a permanent Commission and Court of Human Rights for this purpose, which along with the Council of Europe have their seats in Strasbourg, France. It should be remembered that these institutions are constitutionally distinct from, and must not be confused with, the institutions of the European Union (the European Parliament also in Strasbourg, the Council and Commission in Brussels, and the Court of Justice in Luxembourg).

A full examination of the provisions and procedures under the ECHR is provided in Chapter 2. Before moving on to that, some general points may be made on the implications for Member States participating in international conventions and their influence upon domestic law.

PARTICIPATING IN INTERNATIONAL INSTRUMENTS

Rules relating to international agreements have been codified in the Vienna Convention on the Law of Treaties (concluded 1969, in force 1980). The Convention provides guidance on the conclusion of agreements, which is outlined in the chart opposite.

INFLUENCE UPON DOMESTIC LAW

It is well settled that international law will apply to a State regardless of its domestic law; it cannot plead its own domestic law or constitution as an excuse for breaches of international obligations (Art 27 of the Vienna Convention). Yet the question of whether international law forms a part of domestic law is more complex. There are two contrasting approaches, which may be characterised by two academic schools of thought: 'monism' and 'dualism'.

Monists contend that there is one system of law, with international and domestic laws as but two aspects of that one system. International law is superior, in that it represents a higher set of rules to which domestic law must yield. For example, the US Constitution regards international treaties that bind the US as 'the supreme law of the land' (Art VI, s 2). Similarly, in France and Germany, international law generally takes precedence in domestic law without the need to enact domestic legislation. In this approach, the provisions of international law are sometimes described as 'self-executing'.

Participating in international instruments

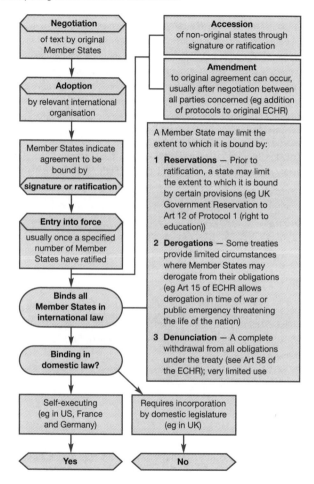

Negotiation
of text by original
Member States

Accession
of non-original states through
signature or ratification

Amendment
to original agreement can occur,
usually after negotiation between
all parties concerned (eg addition
of protocols to original ECHR)

Adoption
by relevant international
organisation

Member States indicate
agreement to be
bound by
signature or ratification

A Member State may limit the
extent to which it is bound by:

1 **Reservations** — Prior to
ratification, a state may limit
the extent to which it is bound
by certain provisions (eg UK
Government Reservation to
Art 12 of Protocol 1 (right to
education))

Entry into force
usually once a specified
number of Member
States have ratified

2 **Derogations** — Some treaties
provide limited circumstances
where Member States may
derogate from their obligations
(eg Art 15 of ECHR allows
derogation in time of war or
public emergency threatening
the life of the nation)

**Binds all
Member States in
international law**

**Binding in
domestic law?**

3 **Denunciation** — A complete
withdrawal from all obligations
under the treaty (see Art 58 of
the ECHR); very limited use

Self-executing
(eg in US, France
and Germany)

Requires incorporation
by domestic legislature
(eg in UK)

Yes

No

Dualists, on the other hand, contend that these two kinds of law are distinct and separate, governing different areas and relationships, and different in substance. International law is inferior, and can only ever become part of domestic law by being incorporated into it by domestic legislation. This is the case in the UK courts, where the legal system is entirely dualist and there are no provisions for international law to be 'self-executing'. So, for example, prior to incorporation of the ECHR, in *Malone v Metropolitan Police Commissioner (No 2)* [1979], Vice Chancellor Megarry stated that 'the [ECHR] is not law here' and as such he had no jurisdiction to declare police tapping of phone calls to be a violation of Art 8 of the ECHR.

The approach adopted by judges in the UK and the position of the ECHR in English law prior to incorporation by the Human Rights Act 1998 is considered more fully in Chapter 3.

A NEW ERA
Whichever approach is taken at the domestic level, the emergence of international human rights law after 1945 was a revolution in the field. In the classical tradition, international law could only deal with the relations between states, not with the rights of individuals. The adoption of the UDHR and its sibling conventions signalled the end of that era.

For a fuller examination of the emergence of international law after 1945 and the text of the most important treaties, see Paul Sieghart, *The International Law of Human Rights* (1983).

You should now be confident that you would be able to tick all of the boxes on the checklist at the beginning of this chapter. To check your knowledge of The origins of human rights law why not visit the companion website and take the Multiple Choice Question test. Check your understanding of the terms and vocabulary used in this chapter with the flashcard glossary.

2

The European Convention on Human Rights

THE INSTITUTIONS AND PROCEDURE

The Council of Europe was established in 1949 and adopted the ECHR in 1950. Section II of the Convention set up a system for application and enforcement. Three institutions were entrusted with the responsibility:

1 the European Commission of Human Rights (set up in 1954);
2 the European Court of Human Rights (ECtHR) (set up in 1959, newly constituted in 1998); and
3 the Committee of Ministers of the Council of Europe, being composed of the ministers for foreign affairs of the Member States.

The Committee of Ministers of the Council of Europe has the responsibility of supervising the execution of the Court's judgments. In 1998 it lost any adjudicative role.

Prior to 1998, the Commission had determined the admissibility of applications. However, with a growing backlog of cases and dissatisfaction at other complexities in procedure, the system for application and enforcement was radically overhauled by Protocol 11, which came into force in November 1998.

Under the new procedure, all decisions on the admissibility and the merits of an application are decided by the ECtHR, a newly constituted, single, full-time court.

The new ECtHR

■ The ECtHR is composed of a number of judges equal to the number of Member States of the Council of Europe (currently 44). There is no restriction on the number of judges of the same nationality.

■ Judges are elected by the Parliamentary Assembly of the Council of Europe for a term of six years.

■ Judges sit on the Court in their individual capacity and do not represent any State.

■ Judges sit in Committees (of three), in Chambers (of seven) and in the Grand Chamber (of 17).

Procedure before the ECtHR

1 Any Contracting State (State application) or individual claiming to be a victim of a violation of the Convention (individual application) may lodge

their complaint directly with the Court in Strasbourg. The right to make an individual application was only recognised by the UK in 1966.

2 Any domestic remedies that are available must be exhausted (Art 35). Only where there is no further court of appeal or where an appeal is certain to fail (eg, strong domestic precedents against the applicant) may an individual lodge an application.

3 The application must be registered at the ECtHR's registry within six months of the final decision of the highest court having jurisdiction within the domestic legal system.

4 After a preliminary examination by an appointed judge rapporteur, the admissibility of an individual application will be decided either by a Committee of three judges or directly by a Chamber of seven. Individual applications which are not declared inadmissible by Committees, along with those that are referred directly to a Chamber by the rapporteur, and state applications, are examined by a Chamber. Chambers determine both admissibility and merits.

5 A Chamber may at any time relinquish jurisdiction in favour of the Grand Chamber where there is a serious question of interpretation of the ECHR or where there is a risk of departing from existing case law. All final judgments of the Court are binding on the respondent states concerned.

6 A case may be terminated by a friendly settlement between the parties at any stage of the proceedings before the Court.

See the diagram overleaf for an outline of the procedure.

Criteria for admissibility
Hurdles for an application:

■ It must not be a matter ruled on and investigated previously.

■ It must relate to a right protected by the Convention.

■ There must be no relevant derogations or reservations by the State concerned.

■ It must relate to an organisation for which a Member State has responsibility.

■ It must not be such as to represent an attack on another's rights (Art 17).

■ It must be plausible, genuine and based on good evidence of violation.

13

Procedure before the ECtHR

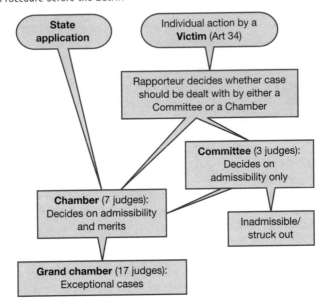

THE STRUCTURE OF THE CONVENTION

Three sections and the protocols

Section I (Arts 1–18) The rights and freedoms	*Protocols 1, 4, 6, 7, 12, 13* Additional rights and freedoms
Section II (Arts 19–51) Establishment of the European Court of Human Rights	*Protocol 11* Restructuring the control machinery
Section III (Arts 52–59) Miscellaneous provisions, eg procedure for reservations, derogations and ratification	*Protocols 2, 3, 5, 8–10* Now defunct: either integrated into main text of Convention or repealed by Protocol 11

Since the ECHR's entry into force, 13 protocols have been adopted. These have expanded the rights and freedoms guaranteed in Section I and have amended the enforcement machinery and procedure in Sections II and III. Note that protocols are only binding on those states that ratify them.

Articles dealing with substantive rights

Article

1 The High Contracting Parties shall secure to everyone within their jurisdiction the rights and freedoms defined in Section I of this Convention

2 Right to life

3 Prohibition of torture

4 Prohibition of slavery and forced labour

5 Right to liberty and security

6 Right to a fair trial

7 No punishment without law (no retrospective law)

8 Right to respect for private and family life

9 Freedom of thought, conscience and religion

10 Freedom of expression

11 Freedom of assembly and association

12 Right to marry

13 Right to an effective remedy

Protocols dealing with substantive rights and UK status as at December 2010

Protocol			UK status
1	(1)	Right to peaceful enjoyment of possessions	in force
	(2)	Right to education	in force (reservation)
	(3)	Right to free elections	in force
4	(1)	Prohibition of imprisonment for debt	signed, not ratified
	(2)	Freedom of movement	signed, not ratified
	(3)	Prohibition of expulsion of nationals	signed, not ratified
	(4)	Prohibition of collective expulsion of aliens	signed, not ratified
6		Abolition of the death penalty	in force
7	(1)	Procedural safeguards relating to expulsion of aliens	not signed
	(2)	Right of appeal in criminal matters	not signed
	(3)	Compensation for wrongful conviction	not signed
	(4)	Right not to be tried or punished twice	not signed
	(5)	Equality between spouses	not signed
12		General prohibition of discrimination (free standing)	not signed
13		Complete abolition of the death penalty	ratified by majority of Council of Europe
14		Amendments to the control system of the convention	in force

Note: Protocols 2, 3, 5, 8, 9, 10 are superseded by Protocol 11 which came into force 1st November 1998, followed by Protocol 14 which has been ratified by every state and entered into force on 1st June 2010

Missing rights

Brief mention may be made of some of the rights not included:

- The ECHR is limited to civil and political rights as opposed to social and economic rights (the European Social Charter does cover such rights but one cannot apply to the ECtHR to have rights under the ESC enforced).

- There is no 'right to know'.

- There is limited right to trial for immigrants and asylum seekers.

- The right to privacy is weak.

- There are no specific rights for children.

- The anti-discrimination article is weak.

Note that Art 14 (prohibition of discrimination) is not a 'free standing' right; it can only be raised in conjunction with another right (eg, the right to respect for private and family life *without discrimination*). The Twelfth Protocol does introduce a free standing right not to be discriminated against. However, the UK has not signed that protocol.

Categories of rights protected

The main civil and political rights in Section I can be divided into three categories.

Absolute 'unqualified' rights

Arts 2, 3, 4(1) and 7:

These rights can never be restricted and are not to be balanced with any public interest arguments.

'Derogable' but 'unqualified' rights

Arts 4(2), 5 and 6:

The State can derogate from these rights in times of public emergency (see Art 15); otherwise, they are unqualified.

Qualified rights

Arts 8–11:

These rights are subject to restriction clauses indicating public interest matters to be taken into account.

INTERPRETATIVE APPROACH AT STRASBOURG

Teleological approach

Strasbourg has given particular regard to the 'object and purpose' of the ECHR (a teleological approach) rather than taking a 'literalistic' approach. The 'object and purpose' has been defined as 'the protection of individual human rights' (see *Soering v UK* [1989]) and the 'promotion of a democratic society' (see *Kjeldsen and Others v Denmark* [1976]), and that democracy should encompass 'pluralism, tolerance and broadmindedness' (see *Handyside v UK* [1976]). This has led the ECtHR into taking an expansive rather than a restrictive approach. For example, in *Golder v UK* [1975] the Court read the right of access to a court into Art 6 (fair trial) despite the absence of clear wording.

The Court has also shown that it regards the ECHR as an evolving document. In *Tyrer v UK* [1978], it stated that the ECHR is an instrument which 'must be interpreted in the light of present day conditions'. Decisions that followed *Tyrer* reflected changed social attitudes to homosexuality in *Dudgeon v UK* [1981] and children born out of wedlock in *Marckx v Belgium* [1979] that would not have existed in 1950.

However, a line should be drawn between judicial interpretation, which is permissible, and judicial legislation, which is not. But where it is clear that standards have moved on since the 1950s, the Court has shown that it will not fight shy of judicial 'creativity'. The importance the Court has attached to the ECHR can be seen in pronouncements that it represents 'the public order of Europe' (*Austria v Italy* [1961]) and that in its positive obligations it is evolving as Europe's constitutional bill of rights (*Ireland v UK* [1978]).

Proportionality

The principle of proportionality is central to the interpretation of the ECHR. Inherent in the whole of the Convention is a search for a balance between the demands of society on the one hand and the fundamental rights of the individual on the other. In weighing such a balance, proportionality requires that a measured and justifiable approach be adopted.

The principle is most commonly invoked in relation to Arts 8–11. These are 'qualified' rights, in that the positive right stated in each of those articles is qualified by restrictions that a State may impose on that right, but only to the extent that is 'necessary in a democratic society' for certain listed public interest purposes. Any restrictions that a State places on these rights 'must be proportionate to the legitimate aim pursued' (see *Handyside v UK*, above).

Margin of appreciation

Another doctrine that plays an important part in interpretation is the 'margin of appreciation'. In basic terms it means that the State is given a certain measure of discretion when it takes an action in the area of a Convention right. To some extent the doctrine pays deference to the expertise of the national authorities. In *Handyside*, a book that had been published elsewhere in Europe was banned by the UK for promoting promiscuity in children. The Court deferred to the State authority's assessment of the moral dangers and found no violation of Art 10(1) (freedom of expression), holding that the State restriction fell within Art 10(2) (permissible State restrictions to the freedom). However, the Court also stated 'that this did not give the contracting states an unlimited power of appreciation'. While a certain margin of appreciation will be granted, any action must still be proportionate.

This can be illustrated by *Dudgeon v UK* [1982], where the Court held that a right to a private life includes a right to private sexual life, and any interference by the State with that right would have to be justified on very strong grounds. See also *Smith and Grady v UK* [1989], the prohibition of homosexuals serving in the armed forces was found to be disproportionate. In *Sunday Times v UK* [1979], the application of a contempt of court order against the *Sunday Times* newspaper for commenting on the thalidomide disaster was also found to be disproportionate.

Some other points on interpretation to note

- There is no doctrine of binding precedent.

- The ECHR is intended to guarantee rights that are practical and effective, not theoretical and illusory (*Artico v Italy* [1980]).

▨ Any limitation imposed upon a right must be prescribed by law:

  ● The citizen must have adequate indication as to the legal rules that apply.
  ● A norm cannot be regarded as sufficiently formulated to be regarded as law.

▨ Article 1 of the Convention has been taken to impose both positive and negative obligations on states. A negative obligation is one that requires the State to abstain from interfering with a right. A positive obligation requires the State to take steps to ensure that a right is protected or secured. See *X and Y v Netherlands* [1985].

STRASBOURG CASE LAW ON THE ARTICLES

The general application of the articles in Strasbourg jurisprudence is illustrated below. The question of how this approach has influenced domestic law in the UK both before and after incorporation by the Human Rights Act (HRA) 1998 is looked at in later chapters.

The illustrations employ a preponderance of cases where the UK is the respondent state for reasons of relevance to domestic application and because the UK has had a considerable number of violations found against it. It should be remembered that in nearly all other European countries, the ECHR has been enshrined in domestic law for some time, or else the state's constitution includes a bill of rights.

> ### Article 1 – Obligation to respect human rights
> The High Contracting Parties shall secure to everyone within their jurisdiction the rights and freedoms defined in Section I of this Convention.

Article 1 defines the obligation of the Member States. Furthermore, Member States are bound in international law by judgments of the ECtHR where they are the respondent. However, there is no direct means of sanctioning a Member State that does not fulfil its obligation, other than perhaps in the case of repeated breach, in which case the State may be expelled from the Council of Europe. Diplomatic pressure, though, is likely to ensure compliance. Most States will modify a practice where a violation has been found. Article 1 was not incorporated into UK law by the HRA 1998; the reasoning behind this decision is examined in Chapter 4.

Article 2 – Right to life

1 Everyone's right to life shall be protected by law. No one shall be deprived of his life intentionally save in the execution of a sentence of a court following his conviction of a crime for which this penalty is provided by law.

2 Deprivation of life shall not be regarded as inflicted in contravention of this article when it results from the use of force which is no more than absolutely necessary:

   a   in defence of any person from unlawful violence;
   b   in order to effect a lawful arrest or to prevent the escape of a person lawfully detained;
   c   in action lawfully taken for the purpose of quelling a riot or insurrection.

Article 2(1) does not prohibit the death penalty. However, note that Protocol 6 abolished the death penalty in peace time (ratified by the UK) and most recently Protocol 13 abolishes the death penalty in wartime. Article 2's interpretation must be guided by recognition of its fundamental importance in the Convention. Its provisions must be strictly construed (*McCann and Others v UK* [1995]).

Does a right to life include a 'right to death' in the form of assisted suicide?

- *Pretty v UK* [2002]: Diane Pretty was dying of motor neurone disease, the final stages of which are distressing and undignified. Although it is not a crime to commit suicide in English law, assistance by her husband would be. The Grand Chamber ruled that no corollary 'right to die', whether at the hands of a third person or with the assistance of a public authority, could be derived from Art 2.

   R (on application of Purdy) v Director of Public Prosecutions [2009] followed on from Pretty and resulted in the DDP being required to publish the facts and circumstances which would be taken into account when deciding whether or not to consent to a prosecution. Note: this does not mean that someone assisting and intending suicide will be immune from prosecution, every case will remain liable to investigation.

Withdrawal of treatment

▨ *NHS Trust A v M; NHS Trust B v H* [2001]: withdrawal of treatment where a patient is in a permanent vegetative state does not infringe the right to life.

Whether an unborn foetus could have Art 2 rights (re abortion)

▨ *Paton v UK* [1981], concerning the abortion of a 10-week-old foetus: there was no breach of Art 2, but it was left open whether this was because the foetus itself was not protected by Art 2 or because the Art 2 right was not absolute in the light of the mother's rights under Art 8.

Circumstances and extent to which lethal force is permissible under Art 2(2)(a), (b) or (c) and duties to investigate

▨ *Kelly v UK* [1993]: soldiers shot dead a joyrider who passed through a checkpoint. The use of force was held to be justifiable and there was no violation of Art 2.

▨ *McCann and Others v UK* [1995]: three unarmed IRA members were shot dead from behind by members of the SAS in Gibraltar; the soldiers said that they feared the suspects were about to detonate a car bomb by remote control. However, these fears proved erroneous, but given the honest belief of the soldiers, their actions did not in themselves give rise to a violation of Art 2(2). In light of the entire operation, though, the three killings did constitute a use of force more than 'absolutely necessary' in violation of Art 2(2). Damages were considered inappropriate given that the terrorists had planned to detonate a car bomb on a subsequent date.

▨ *Jordan v UK* [2001], re the right to have a death investigated: the applicant's unarmed son was shot by the Royal Ulster Constabulary. The national authorities failed to carry out a prompt and effective investigation into the circumstances of the death. The ECtHR held that an effective official investigation following a death was implicit in the Art 2 right to life. A similar decision was given in *McShane v UK* [2002].

▨ *Edwards v UK* [2002]: putting Edwards in a prison cell with an individual who had a history of violent outbursts and assaults, including a previous assault on a cellmate in prison, without sufficient precautions, disclosed a breach of the State's obligation to protect Edwards' life. The Court found a violation of Art 2.

Extraterritoriality

R (on the application of Gentle) v Prime Minister [2008] UKHL 20 – considered substantive obligations on Government under Art 2 regarding the legality of the Government actions within a framework of International Law, specifically the legality of military activities in the Iraq war and resultant procedural obligation under Art 2 to establish an effective and procedural investigation into fatalities. Appeal dismissed.

R (Al-Skeini and others) v Secretary of State for Defence (The Redress Trust and others intervening) [2007] UKHL 26; [2008] 1 AC 153. Case brought by the families of five Iraqi civilians killed by British troops, and considered the application of convention rights to UK public authorities outside the UK. Court found wherever UK had jurisdiction in respect of Art 1, ECHR rights could apply.

Clash with Art 10

- *Thompson and Venables v News Group Newspapers and Others* [2001], the Bulger case: in another example of the horizontal effect of the HRA 1998, a permanent injunction was granted to protect the boys' new identities. Their Art 2 rights outweighed any Art 10 rights the newspapers might have in publishing details about the boys.

Article 3 – Prohibition of torture

No one shall be subjected to torture or to inhuman or degrading treatment or punishment.

Article 3 is intended to protect an individual's dignity and physical integrity. It provides absolute protection against treatment falling within its scope, consequently case law is largely concerned with defining what constitutes

(a) torture

(b) inhuman treatment

(c) degrading treatment.

It should be noted that this is an area where the 'living instrument' aspect of the convention is very apparent.

The State is never able to argue that such treatment has local acceptability, or that it served as a deterrent, or that there were reasons justifying it in the particular case. Moreover, no derogation by the State under Art 15 of the Convention is possible.

- *East African Asian v UK* [1973]: where different immigration controls into the UK were exercised according to ethnic background, the ECtHR held that publicly to single out a group of persons for differential treatment on the basis of race may constitute a special form of affront to human dignity and might therefore be capable of constituting degrading treatment under Art 3.

- *Ireland v UK* [1976]: the ECtHR ruled that interrogation methods used on IRA suspects fell within the meaning of degrading treatment. These included continuous standing for over 20 hours, hooding, and deprivation of sleep, food and drink.

- *Tyrer v UK* [1978]: Tyler, who was aged 15, was birched by a prefect. Birching *per se* was ruled not to be degrading, as the treatment must reach a certain level to be so. However, the victim was made to undress; in those circumstances the treatment was a violation of Art 3. Similarly in *Costello-Roberts v UK* [1993], corporal punishment as opposed to ordinary physical punishment may violate Art 3.

- *Askoy v Turkey* [1996]: in this case the applicant was strung up in a cell, blindfolded and electrodes attached to his genitals, the Court held that this clearly amounted to torture.

- *Aydin v Turkey* [1997] found that rape by a State official could constitute torture.

- *Selmouni v France* [2000]: treatment while in police custody amounted to torture where the applicant was subjected to prolonged assaults, including being assaulted with a truncheon, being urinated over, and being threatened with blowlamps and a syringe.

- *Keenan v UK* [2001]: a violation was found due to disciplinary punishment given to a mentally disordered prisoner, known to be a suicide risk, who committed suicide. The punishment constituted degrading treatment within the meaning of Art 3.

▓ *Price v UK* [2001]: a severely disabled person's detention with grossly inadequate provisions in police custody constituted degrading treatment in contravention of Art 3. While not present in the instant case, one factor the Court was required to consider was whether the treatment was intended to humiliate.

▓ *Z v UK* [2001]: where a public authority failed to protect children from serious ill treatment and neglect by their parents for four and a half years, the ECtHR held that there was a positive obligation to take steps to prevent such treatment; so there was a violation of Art 3.

Evidence obtained under torture
A v Others v Secretary of State for the Home Department [2005]. Court considered that although the Secretary of State did not act unlawfully, the judicial supervision by the commission would require express statutory wording in order to override the exclusionary rule concerning evidence obtained under torture. Therefore, if not accepted by the courts it cannot be accepted by the Commission.

Prison conditions
▓ *Napier v The Scottish Ministers* [2001]: the Court of Session ruled that prison conditions violated Art 3 rights.

Life sentences for mentally ill offenders
▓ *R v Drew* [2002]: the Court of Appeal held that there was no violation of Art 3 or 5 in the imposition of a life sentence on a mentally ill offender where the making of a hospital order would provide insufficient security to the public.

Deportation
Considerable current debate revolves around the possible breach of Art 3 in relation to deporting people to their country of origin where they may face degrading treatment, torture or death.

▓ *Jabari v Turkey* [2000]: the ECtHR held that deportation of an Iranian female refugee would breach her Art 3 rights. No investigation had been carried out of her allegations that she would face being stoned to death or flogged in Iran for adultery.

- *Soering v UK* [1989]: the ECtHR held that to take the decision to extradite an individual to the US, without receiving formal assurance that the death penalty would neither be sought nor imposed, would amount to a violation of Art 3.

- *Chahal v UK* [1997]: the Court held that where a militant Sikh established substantial grounds for belief that he would suffer a real risk of ill treatment if deported to India, his Art 3 guarantees were absolute and could not be balanced against a threat to national security. (See also below in relation to Art 5.)

- *D v UK* [1997]: a drug smuggler suffering from AIDS was apprehended whilst entering illegally into the UK with a quantity of drugs. On completion of his sentence in the UK he was due to be deported to St Kitts. By the time of the ECtHR decision, he was in the advanced stages of a terminal illness. It was accepted in court that his life expectancy would be reduced without the medication he received in the UK. The Court held that to remove the applicant to St Kitts would violate Art 3.

- *Bensaid v UK* [2001]: the Court held that there was no violation where the Home Secretary made a decision to deport an overstayer suffering from schizophrenia.

Article 4 – Prohibition of slavery and forced labour

1 No one shall be held in slavery or servitude.

2 No one shall be required to perform forced or compulsory labour.

3 For the purpose of this article the term 'forced or compulsory labour' shall not include:

   a any work required to be done in the ordinary course of detention imposed according to the provisions of Article 5 of this Convention or during conditional release from such detention;

   b any service of a military character or, in case of conscientious objectors in countries where they are recognised, service exacted instead of compulsory military service;

   c any service exacted in case of an emergency or calamity threatening the life or well-being of the community;

   d any work or service which forms part of normal civic obligations.

The Court has considered the application of Art 4 on only a few occasions and has never found a violation. The article is most frequently invoked by individuals who complain about work that they were required to do while in detention, or services that the state required them to provide to others.

In *Van de Mussele v Belgium* [1982], a lawyer claimed that forced *pro bono* work was in violation of Art 4; the ECtHR rejected the claim. Forced or compulsory labour must be

(a) against a person's will;

(b) the obligation must be unjust or oppressive;

(c) it must constitute an avoidable hardship.

Conscientious objectors, in countries where there is compulsory military service have also been considered under Art 4, see *Johansen v Norway* [1985], *Spottl v Austria* [1996], where a conscientious objector forced to carry out civilian rather than military service was not a violation of Art 4.

Article 5 – Right to liberty and security

1 Everyone has the right to liberty and security of person. No one shall be deprived of his liberty save in the following cases and in accordance with a procedure prescribed by law:

   a   the lawful detention of a person after conviction by a competent court;

   b   the lawful arrest or detention of a person for non-compliance with the lawful order of a court or in order to secure the fulfilment of any obligation prescribed by law;

   c   the lawful arrest or detention of a person effected for the purpose of bringing him before the competent legal authority on reasonable suspicion of having committed an offence or when it is reasonably considered necessary to prevent his committing an offence or fleeing after having done so;

   d   the detention of a minor by lawful order for the purpose of educational supervision or his lawful detention for the purpose of bringing him before the competent legal authority;

e   the lawful detention of persons for the prevention of the spreading
     of infectious diseases, of persons of unsound mind, alcoholics or
     drug addicts or vagrants;

f   the lawful arrest or detention of a person to prevent his effecting an
     unauthorised entry into the country or of a person against whom
     action is being taken with a view to deportation or extradition.

2   Everyone who is arrested shall be informed promptly, in a language
     which he understands, of the reasons for his arrest and of any charge
     against him.

3   Everyone arrested or detained in accordance with the provisions of
     paragraph 1(c) of this article shall be brought promptly before a judge
     or other officer authorised by law to exercise judicial power and shall
     be entitled to trial within a reasonable time or to release pending trial.
     Release may be conditioned by guarantees to appear for trial.

4   Everyone who is deprived of his liberty by arrest or detention shall be
     entitled to take proceedings by which the lawfulness of his detention
     shall be decided speedily by a court and his release ordered if the
     detention is not lawful.

5   Everyone who has been the victim of arrest or detention in contraven-
     tion of the provisions of this article shall have an enforceable right to
     compensation.

Article 5 is the subject of much ECtHR case law. The article's underlying aim is 'to ensure that no one should be dispossessed of [their] liberty in an arbitrary fashion' (*Engel v The Netherlands* [1976]). The most common breaches raised are under para (1), which requires there to be a legal basis for detention as outlined in sub-paras (a)–(f). Paragraph (3) requires that upon arrest a person must be brought promptly before a court, and therefore limits the time he may be held without charge. Paragraph (4) requires such person to have effective legal means to query the basis of detention and that any such decision should be reached speedily.

Pre-trial detention

■ *Stogmuller v Austria* [1969], re bail pending trial: the ECtHR stated that it will assess the reasonableness of the grounds for serious departure from the respect afforded to individuals implicit in the presumption of innocence.

■ *Letellier v France* [1991]: the Court indicated that the fear of absconding or witness intimidation as a basis for keeping a defendant on remand will not be justified where detention is for an inordinate period (in this case, two years and nine months).

■ *Caballero v UK* [2000]: the automatic denial of bail under s 25 of the Criminal Justice and Public Order Act 1994 for offences of homicide or rape where the defendant has previous convictions for those offences was held to be a violation of Art 5. The UK Government had already conceded the point and s 25 was duly amended by the Crime and Disorder Act 1998. There is now a discretion to grant bail where 'exceptional circumstances' justify it.

■ *Jordan v UK* [2001]: the Court found violations of Art 5(3) and (5) for detention of a soldier under close arrest.

Life sentences/Parole Board and sentence reviews

■ *Oldham v UK* [2001]: the applicant, having been sentenced to discretionary life imprisonment, complained that a two year delay between his Parole Board reviews was unreasonable. The Court held that the question of whether the applicant's continued detention was lawful was not decided 'speedily' within the meaning of Art 5(4) and that 'speedily' also implies that, where an automatic review of the lawfulness of detention has been instituted, decisions must follow at 'reasonable intervals'. See also *Hirst v UK* [2001].

■ *Curley v UK* [2001]: the Court found violations of para (4) re the failure to review a sentence tariff speedily.

■ *T and V v UK* [2000]: the Court held that the fixing of a tariff (or minimum term) for young persons convicted of murder and detained at Her Majesty's pleasure is a sentencing exercise, such that the procedure whereby the tariff was fixed by the Home Secretary constituted a violation of Art 6(1). The Court concluded that the failure to refer their case to the Parole Board amounted to a violation of Art 5. The Criminal Justice Act 2003 now requires the minimum term of mandatory life sentences to be set by the trial judge in open court. This applies equally to sentences of detention during Her Majesty's pleasure.

▨ *Stafford v UK* [2002]: Stafford was given a mandatory life sentence in 1967 for murder and was released on licence in 1979. In July 1994 he was convicted of forging cheques and passports and sentenced to six years' imprisonment. In 1997 the Parole Board recommended his release, but, despite it being accepted that S was no longer dangerous or violent, the Home Secretary refused to do so. He continued S's detention by revocation of the life licence in relation to the original mandatory life sentence. The ECtHR held that Art 5(1) and (4) were breached, stating that the lawfulness of the detention after 1 July 1997 should have been periodically reviewed by a court and not by a politician.

Mental health restrictions

▨ *X v Belgium* [1972]: indefinite detention is compatible with Art 5(1)(e) providing it is attended by the guarantees required by para (4) (query/ review).

▨ *Ashingdane v UK* [1985]: the Court held that the detention of persons of unsound mind is required to be in a hospital, clinic, or other appropriate institution authorised for the detention of such persons.

▨ *Johnson v UK* [1996]: the applicant had been detained under mental health provisions in relation to a number of assaults committed by him. Subsequently he was found to be no longer suffering from mental illness, but since no suitable accommodation was available his detention was continued. The Court found a violation of Art 5(1).

▨ *HL v UK* [2004]: the Court found a violation of Art 5(4) in respect of the confinement as an 'informal patient' of a person with a mental disorder who was 'compliant' but incapable of either giving or refusing consent. The House of Lords had earlier ruled that the applicant's detention was lawful in so far as it was justified by the common law doctrine of necessity (*R v Bournewood Community and Mental Health NHS Trust, ex p L* [1999]). The Court was struck in particular by the lack of procedural safeguards applicable to this type of confinement, which it furthermore qualified as a 'deprivation of liberty'.

Detention of terrorists

The detention of terrorists in Northern Ireland has given rise to a considerable amount of case law at Strasbourg. In general, the ECtHR has allowed States a considerable margin of appreciation where suspected terrorists are detained.

- ▣ *Murray v UK* [1995]: the Court considered two factors to be in the balance – 'the responsibility of an elected government in a democratic society to protect its citizens and its institutions against threats posed by organised terrorism and ... the special problems involved in the arrest and detention of persons suspected of terrorist-linked offences'. Consequently in *Murray*, despite alleged breaches of Arts 5 and 8 for procedural irregularities in detention and the retention of private documents, no violations were found.

Derogations

Article 15 permits a State to derogate from Art 5 in times of war or other public emergency threatening the life of the nation. Previously, the UK entered a derogation in relation to Art 5(3) in response to the judgment in *Brogan v UK* [1988].

- ▣ *Brogan v UK* [1988]: the ECtHR held that detention of a suspected terrorist on the authority of the Secretary of State (without being brought before an appropriate judicial authority) for four days and six hours under the Prevention of Terrorism (Temporary Provisions) Act 1984 was incompatible with para (3).

The UK Government has since implemented Sched 8 to the Terrorism Act 2000, which introduces a judicial element, and the derogation has been withdrawn.

The UK entered a further derogation to Art 5(1) in relation to the detention of suspected international terrorists under the Anti-terrorism, Crime and Security Act 2001. The Act provided for an extended power to arrest and detain without the need to be brought before a court. The power applied where it was intended to remove or deport a suspected terrorist from the UK but where removal or deportation was prevented, for example where removal to their own country might result in treatment contrary to Art 3 of the Convention. However, in *A & Others v Secretary of State for the Home Department* [2004] the House of Lords ruled that the measures for indefinite detention contained in the ATCSA 2001 did not satisfy the criteria for derogating under Art 15, in that the measures were not 'strictly required' by the exigencies of the situation. The government has since repealed the measures and the derogation has been withdrawn.

Article 6 – Right to a fair trial

1 In the determination of his civil rights and obligations or of any criminal charge against him, everyone is entitled to a fair and public hearing within a reasonable time by an independent and impartial tribunal established by law. Judgment shall be pronounced publicly but the press and public may be excluded from all or part of the trial in the interests of morals, public order or national security in a democratic society, where the interests of juveniles or the protection of the private life of the parties so require, or to the extent strictly necessary in the opinion of the court in special circumstances where publicity would prejudice the interests of justice.

2 Everyone charged with a criminal offence shall be presumed innocent until proved guilty according to law.

3 Everyone charged with a criminal offence has the following minimum rights:

   a to be informed promptly, in a language which he understands and in detail, of the nature and cause of the accusation against him;
   b to have adequate time and facilities for the preparation of his defence;
   c to defend himself in person or through legal assistance of his own choosing or, if he has not sufficient means to pay for legal assistance, to be given it free when the interests of justice so require;
   d to examine or have examined witnesses against him and to obtain the attendance and examination of witnesses on his behalf under the same conditions as witnesses against him;
   e to have the free assistance of an interpreter if he cannot understand or speak the language used in court.

Article 6 contains the fundamental principle which underpins the ECHR, namely the fair administration of justice. It is the most commonly raised article. It guarantees, first, access to a court for the determination of a person's civil rights and obligations or of any criminal charge against him (*Golder v UK*) and, secondly, procedural fairness in the course of those proceedings.

Meaning of 'civil rights and obligations'

There is broad interpretation, generally based on definitions in domestic law, but the ECtHR retains discretion to employ an autonomous Convention interpretation which is not confined to traditional private law rights, as recognised in the domestic law, but extends to rights and obligations of a civil 'character' (*Ringeisen v Austria (No 1)* [1971]).

Meaning of 'criminal charge'

- *Lutz v Germany* [1987]: the Court will look behind any domestic classification, and ask whether the act in the proceedings is by its nature 'criminal' from the point of view of the Convention, or is open to sanction which belongs in general to the 'criminal' sphere. See also *Campbell and Fell v UK* [1984], where Art 6 was held to apply to disciplinary proceedings before a Board of Prison Visitors. See, similarly, *Ezeh and Connors v UK* [2003].

Criminal charge

- *Matthewson v The Scottish Ministers* [2001]: accusations of breaching prison rules did not amount to a criminal charge, and Art 6 guarantees did not apply. In *Re M* [2001], secure accommodation orders, though not criminal proceedings, nonetheless were subject to Art 6 guarantees.

- *R v Manchester Crown Court ex p McCann* [2002]: the purpose of Anti-Social Behaviour Orders (ASBOs) is preventive and not punitive and since such proceedings does not involve the determination of a criminal charge, they were not classified as criminal for the purposes of Art 6.

Access to law/legal advice

- *Golder v UK* [1975]: a convicted prisoner wished to bring proceedings in defamation against a prison officer. The Prison Rules effectively prevented him from consulting a solicitor. The Court held that the restriction constituted a serious impediment to the right of access to the courts and was therefore incompatible with Art 6(1).

- *Airey v Ireland* [1979], re legal aid: the applicant had commenced complex proceedings for marital separation but could not afford representation. The Court found a violation of Art 6(1) in that appearing in person did not provide the applicant with effective access to law and in such circumstances the State ought to provide the assistance of a lawyer.

▨ *Ashingdane v UK* [1985]: it was held that the right of access is not absolute, but any restrictions must not be so as to impair 'the very essence of the right'.

▨ *Magee v UK* [2000]: a violation was found due to refusal of access to a solicitor for 48 hours, and in *Averill v UK* [2000] due to refusal of access for 24 hours. In *Magee*, the applicant, a suspected terrorist, was held in 'austere' conditions for 48 hours without access to a solicitor, and during this time made a confession which formed the basis of his conviction. The ECtHR held that 'to deny access to a lawyer for such a long period and in a situation where the rights of the defence were irretrievably prejudiced is … incompatible with the rights of the accused under Article 6'.

▨ *Brennan v UK* [2001]: the right of access to a solicitor could be subject to restriction for good cause. It was necessary to ascertain whether the restriction had deprived the applicant of a fair hearing. In this case, a police presence during a consultation with a solicitor was held to violate Art 6.

Evidence

▨ In *R v A* [2001] the House of Lords considered s 41 of the Youth Justice and Criminal Evidence Act, which, in sexual offence cases, restricts the cross examination of complainants about previous sexual activity. A literal interpretation of the section would prohibit a defendant cross-examining a complainant about previous consensual activity between the parties where consent was in issue. Despite the obvious meaning of the provisions, the House of Lords ruled that evidence necessary to ensure a fair trial under Art 6 would nonetheless be admissible, thereby avoiding a declaration under s 4.

Blanket restrictions

▨ *Stubbings v UK* [1997]: examined the restriction of access by virtue of the Limitation Act 1980. The Court ruled that the state could limit access provided the limitations pursued a legitimate objective, were proportionate and did not remove the essence of the right.

▨ Immunity from prosecution has been examined as a denial of access. Violations of Art 6(1) were found in *Osman v UK* [2000] (blanket immunity of police from negligence claims in respect of investigations) and in *McElhinny v Ireland* [2002] (State immunity protecting a British soldier from being sued for personal injury).

Procedural guarantees

- *CG v UK* [2002]: the applicant alleged that the trial judge had frequently interrupted and hectored her defence counsel during his cross-examination of prosecution witnesses and during her evidence in chief in her theft trial. The ECtHR held that although the judge had intervened in an excessive and undesirable manner, that had not amounted to a breach of Art 6 rights to a fair trial. It was significant that defence counsel had been able to make an uninterrupted closing speech lasting 45 minutes, and that the essence of the defence had been restated by the judge.

The applicable test of whether a trial is independent and impartial is whether, regardless of actual bias, the public is 'reasonably entitled' to entertain doubts over the independence or impartiality of the tribunal (*Campbell and Fell v UK* [1984]) or whether there are 'legitimate grounds for fearing' that the tribunal is not independent or impartial (*McGonnell v UK* [2000]). The latter case involved the Bailiff of Guernsey, who has executive, legislative and judicial functions. The Court held that even though there was no actual bias, in a planning matter where the Bailiff was already involved by virtue of his legislative role, it was a violation of Art 6 for him to adjudicate on the same matter in his judicial capacity.

- *T and V v UK* [2000]: the ECtHR held that executive involvement in sentencing is a breach of the independence requirement in Art 6(1). Also, re the right to participate effectively in criminal proceedings, it was held that requirements included being able to understand the evidence and argument, to instruct lawyers, and to give evidence.

- *Granger v UK* [1990], re equality of arms: the applicant's liberty was at stake but he could only represent himself while the Crown was represented by high counsel. The ECtHR held that there was a violation.

- *Jespers v Belgium* [1978]: the Commission held that the 'equality of arms' principle imposes on prosecuting and investigating authorities an obligation to disclose any material in their possession, or to which they could gain access, which may assist the accused. See similarly *Rowe and Others v UK* [2000].

- *Delic v Croatia* [2002]: the court found that there had been a violation of Art 6(1) in respect of nine sets of proceedings which had lasted up to four and a half years, and hence fell outside the remit of 'within a reasonable time', and awarded the applicant damages.

Evidence

- *Condron v UK* [2000], re the right to silence and adverse inferences: the ECtHR stated that the right to silence was not absolute but, 'like the privilege against self-incrimination, [it] lay at the heart of the notion of a fair procedure under Article 6, [and] particular caution was required before a domestic court could invoke an accused's silence against him'.

- *Saunders v UK* [1994], otherwise known as 'the Guinness affair': the Court considered the matter of privilege against self-incrimination. It held that the admission in evidence at the applicant's trial of transcripts of interviews with Department of Trade and Industry inspectors violated Art 6(1), since at the time of the interrogation the applicant was under a duty to answer the questions, which was enforceable by criminal proceedings for contempt. This decision was followed in *IJL and Others v UK* [2000].

- *Heaney and McGuinness v Ireland* [2001]: the Court held there to be violations of Art 6(1) and (2) as the privilege against self-incrimination was violated by a provision stipulating that a suspected terrorist would be liable to a prison sentence where he failed to give a full account of his movements to the police.

- *Austria v Italy* [1963], re unlawfully obtained evidence: the admission of a confession obtained as a result of ill treatment was held inevitably to violate Art 6. However, in *Khan v UK* [2000], the Court held that the admission of evidence obtained by a covert listening device was not a violation of the article. The central question was whether the proceedings as a whole were fair. There was a violation of Art 8. A similar conclusion was found in *PG and JH v UK* [2001].

- *Philips v UK* [2002]: this case tested the basis of the presumption of innocence and whether the onus of proof can be reversed. There was a rebuttable presumption under the Drug Trafficking Act 1994 (provisions now under the Proceeds of Crime Act 2002) that all property held by a person convicted of a drug trafficking offence within the preceding six years represents the proceeds of drug trafficking; this presumption was challenged. The court held that Art 6 did not apply, the conviction had been secured, and the confiscation was part of the sentencing process. In other circumstances, the ECtHR has held that Art 6(2) does not impose an absolute prohibition on reverse burden provisions. In *X v UK* [1972], the Commission upheld a rebuttable presumption that a man proved to be living with or controlling a prostitute was presumed to be living off immoral earnings.

Article 7 – No punishment without law

1 No one shall be held guilty of any criminal offence on account of any act or omission which did not constitute a criminal offence under national or international law at the time when it was committed. Nor shall a heavier penalty be imposed than the one that was applicable at the time the criminal offence was committed.

2 This article shall not prejudice the trial and punishment of any person for any act or omission which, at the time when it was committed, was criminal according to the general principles of law recognised by civilised nations.

Article 7 creates a non-derogable prohibition on the retrospective application of the criminal law. It applies only to criminal law and is already a principle of UK domestic law.

It would seem at face value to be a straightforward concept that no one should be held to account for doing something which was not an offence when they did it, which is already a principle of UK domestic law. See *Waddington v Miah* [1974]. However, it is necessary for the common law to have an aspect of flexibility whereby it is able to take into account the changing values of society, and this is very much the aspect of the ECHR as a 'living instrument'.

It is worth noting that the Article states that a criminal offence is one under either national or international law (which gives a right to prosecute someone for a crime which was not illegal under their domestic law at the time, so long as it was prohibited by international law).

Legislation: Prevention or Penalty?
■ *Welch v UK* [1995]: the applicant committed a drugs offence in 1986 and was convicted in 1988. His sentence included a confiscation order pursuant

to provisions in the Drug Trafficking Offences Act 1986, which came into force in 1987. The Court held that there had been a violation of Art 7(1).

▪ *Ibbotson v UK* [1999] Crim LR 153 was originally convicted for possession of indecent and obscene material. He was released in 1997, and later that same year the Sex Offenders Act came into force, which required those convicted of sexual offences to register with the Police. This, he claimed, imposed on him an order which had not existed at the time of his offending, thereby breaching his Article 7 rights. The ECtHR held that the registration requirement was preventative rather than punitive, since the aim was that inclusion on the register might dissuade an individual from reoffending. Welch was considered, but the Court held that the requirement of merely registering did not actually amount to a penalty.

The common law

▪ *SW and CR v UK* [1995], re the common law: Art 7 allows for the 'gradual clarification' of the rules of criminal liability from case to case, provided the developments are consistent with the essence of the offence and could reasonably be foreseen. Thus the Court held that the removal of the marital rape exemption by the House of Lords did not amount to a retrospective change in the elements of the offence.

Legal certainty

This gulf between the two aspects of certainty and flexibility within the law is resolved by the suggestion by the ECtHR that if the development of the law is foreseeable, then it will automatically be regarded as being fair and will not conflict with Article 7. This may be seen in the case of *Kokkinakis v Greece* [1993] 17 EHRR 397 where Greek law, the court considered, was accessible to Mr Kokkinakis, and would therefore be considered to be clear and understandable. One might compare this with the case of *Hashman and Harrup v UK* [2000] 30 EHRR 241, where the court order of *contra bonos mores* (against good morals) was considered to be unclear to those on whom the penalty was imposed, and inexact as to what, exactly, they should or should not do.

War crimes

The exception created by Art 7(2) allows national and international legislation to be enacted to punish war crimes, such as torture and genocide, at a time subsequent to their commission. The logic behind this is that they would have been criminal according to the standards of their time. See the War Crimes Act 1991 in the UK.

Article 8 – Right to respect for private and family life

1 Everyone has the right to respect for his private and family life, his home and his correspondence.

2 There shall be no interference by a public authority with the exercise of this right except such as is in accordance with the law and is necessary in a democratic society in the interests of national security, public safety or the economic well-being of the country, for the prevention of disorder or crime, for the protection of health or morals, or for the protection of the rights and freedoms of others.

As the article states, the areas covered are private and family life, home and correspondence. These areas tend to overlap and the use of 'private' life encompasses a broad definition. Two main areas arise: protection from arbitrary interference by the State and respect for an individual's private life and relationships. It is a qualified right, with which the State may only interfere in the pursuit of legitimate aims 'necessary in a democratic society' as listed in para (2). In addition to refraining from interfering, the State may also have positive obligations to ensure that Art 8 rights are respected.

Private life

■ *Costello-Roberts v UK* [1993], re personal development: three whacks of a slipper did not have sufficiently serious effects on the applicant's physical or moral integrity to fall within the scope of the prohibition contained in Art 8.

■ *Gaskin v UK* [1990], re personal information: the protection of the confidentiality of contributors to a personal file relating to the applicant's childhood in care and possible issues of ill treatment was a valid 'rights of others' exception under para (2), provided there was a proper balance weighed with the applicant's right of access.

■ *Dudgeon v UK* [1982], re the right to a choice of sexual relations: the Court held that prohibition under Northern Ireland legislation of homosexual conduct carried out in private between consenting adults (over the age of 21) is an interference with the right to respect for private life and was not justified as necessary in a democratic society. In *Smith v UK* [1999], S and others were administratively discharged from the armed forces on the basis of their homosexuality. Despite arguments being accepted in earlier cases regarding 'operational difficulties' of homosexuals in the armed forces, the Court held here that the investigations, interviews and discharges amounted to an 'exceptional intrusion' into the applicants' private lives, and was a violation of Art 8.

- *Sunday Times v UK* [1979]: the Court looked into the matter of balancing Art 8 with Art 10 when considering limiting protection from press intrusions into private affairs. This arises owing to the need to balance the individual's private interests against the right to freedom of expression and the freedom of the press, which the Court described as an 'essential foundation of a democratic society'. As regards topical domestic developments, see Chapter 5 below.

- *Campbell v UK* [1992], re correspondence: it was held that the supervision of prisoners' letters is not *per se* a breach of Art 8, but reading an applicant's communications with his solicitor was a breach.

- *Von Hannover v Germany* [2004]: the applicant, Princess Caroline of Monaco, had been only partly successful in the German courts with her application for an injunction to prevent tabloid magazines publishing photographs, taken without her knowledge and showing her going about her daily business outside her home. The domestic courts had accepted that 'figures of contemporary society' were entitled to respect for their private life even outside their home, but only if they had retired to a 'secluded place' where it was objectively clear to everyone that they wanted to be alone. The applicant had been successful with regard to photographs showing her with her male friend at the far end of a restaurant courtyard but unsuccessful with regard to the publication of photographs showing her in a 'non-isolated place'. In finding a violation of Art 8, the Court placed emphasis on the fact that the photographs and accompanying commentaries had been published for no other purpose than to satisfy curiosity and the publication had not contributed to any debate of general interest to society, in the proper sense of that notion. It thus held that the State had failed in its positive obligation to ensure the effective protection of the applicant's private life.

Surveillance/police interference

- *Klass v FRG* [1978]: it was held that telephone tapping constituted an inter-ference with private life, but could be justified as being in the interests of national security provided sufficient controls were in place.

- *Malone v UK* [1984]: the Court made it clear that any interference by way of covert phone tapping would have to be in 'accordance with law' to satisfy Art 8(2). The Court implied that there had to be protection against arbitrary interferences by public authorities with the rights in Art 8.

- *Halford v UK* [1997]: the applicant, who had failed to secure promotion, had brought sex discrimination proceedings against the Merseyside Police Authority. There was a reasonable likelihood that her office phone calls had been intercepted. No lawful procedure appeared to have been followed and therefore the court found a violation of Art 8(2).

- *PG and JH v UK* [2002]: the Court held that covert listening devices placed by the police in a private residence and later in the police station cell were in violation of Art 8 as there was no statutory regulation of the use of covert listening devices in these ways.

- *Armstrong v UK* [2002]: the UK accepted that covert surveillance carried out by police before the introduction of the statutory scheme in the Police Act 1997 and before the controls of such surveillance were augmented by the Regulation of Investigatory Powers Act 2000 violated Arts 8 and 13 of the ECHR.

- *McLeod v UK* [1999]: police entry into a private home was held to be a violation.

- *R v Loveridge and Others* [2001]: the police filmed the defendants at a magistrates' court in order to link them to other CCTV pictures taken during the course of a robbery. The Court of Appeal ruled that the filming breached the defendants' Art 8 rights.

- *R v Mason and Others* [2002]: the Court of Appeal held that tapes from covertly recorded conversations of suspects in police cells were admissible in evidence. The arrests had been lawful and there was no bad faith on the part of the police. A breach of Art 8 did not necessarily render the evidence inadmissible.

Family life/home

Note that Art 8 does not confer any right to be provided with a home, or a positive obligation to provide alternative accommodation of an applicant's choosing (*Burton v UK* [1996]).

Gypsy way of life

■ *Clarke v Secretary of State for Transport, Local Government and the Regions* [2002]: the Court of Appeal held that where Art 8 of the Convention was engaged and it had been shown that a person held certain cultural values or beliefs such that he was opposed to living in conventional housing, it was not sufficient for a local authority to rely on the fact that conventional housing had been offered but refused; it was necessary that the personal circumstances of the individual concerned be considered and weighed against planning considerations.

■ *Hatton and Others v UK* [2001], re noise pollution: residents surrounding Heathrow complained of increased noise from night flights. The Court held that although neither the airport nor aircraft were owned or controlled by the Government, the State did have a duty to take reasonable and appropriate steps to uphold the residents' rights. A balance had to be struck between the interests of the residents and benefits to the regional and national economy. A fair balance was not struck and therefore there was a violation of Art 8.

■ *P, C and S v UK* [2002]: a domestic High Court ruled that a newly born baby could be freed for adoption on the basis that the mother represented a serious risk to the child. The mother had a previous conviction for mistreatment of an earlier child (in the US) and continued to suffer from psychological problems likely to endanger her subsequent child. The ECtHR held that the removal of the child at birth from the parent and the lack of legal representation during proceedings disclosed breaches of Arts 8 and 6.

Retention of DNA samples

■ *R (S) v Chief Constable of South Yorkshire* [2004]: the House of Lords ruled that the retention by the police of DNA samples of suspects after they had fulfilled their purpose did not violate Art 8, provided data was destroyed in cases which it turned out should never have been initiated.

Deportation

■ *R v Secretary of State ex p Mahmood* [2001]: the Court of Appeal upheld the Secretary of State's decision to dismiss an application for review of an illegal entrant's removal from the UK. The individual had been married for some two years to a woman resident in the UK who had borne him two children. The court ruled that it was a reasonable decision in that the interference with Art 8 rights was justified under Art 8(2) by the legitimate aim pursued.

■ *R (Samaroo) v Secretary of State for the Home Department* [2001]: where a decision to deport someone is taken, there must be a fair balance struck between the legitimate aim pursued and the individual's Convention rights. In the circumstances, the serious nature of the drug trafficking offence committed by the individual concerned prevented a violation of Art 8 being found.

Positive obligations?

Where a State has failed in its positive duty to deal with interferences with an individual's Art 8 rights, a 'fair balance has to be struck between the competing interests of the individual and of the community as a whole' (*Powell and Rayner v UK* [1990]).

■ *Lopez Ostra v Spain* [1995]: the State was held to have violated Art 8 by failing to deal with an unlicensed waste treatment plant which was emitting fumes close to the applicant's home.

■ *Botta v Italy* [1998]: no violation of Art 8 was found in not providing disabled access to a beach from a holiday residence.

Transsexuals

■ *Sheffield (Kristina) v UK* [1998]: the UK refused to amend its system of registering births so as to permit post-operative transsexuals to record their new sexual identity. The Court held that there was no violation of Art 8. But more recently, in joined cases *I v UK*; *Goodwin v UK* [2002], the Court reached a different conclusion, holding that rights under Arts 8 and 12 were breached where domestic law did not permit a post-operative male to female transsexual to change her birth certificate nor marry her male partner. Similar breaches occurred where domestic law did not permit the transsexual to be treated as a woman for national insurance or pension purposes. The Gender Recognition Act 2004 now provides transsexual people with legal recognition in their acquired gender.

Article 9 – Freedom of thought, conscience and religion

1   Everyone has the right to freedom of thought, conscience and religion; this right includes freedom to change his religion or belief and freedom, either alone or in community with others and in public or private, to manifest his religion or belief, in worship, teaching, practice and observance.

2   Freedom to manifest one's religion or beliefs shall be subject only to such limitations as are prescribed by law and are necessary in a democratic society in the interests of public safety, for the protection of public order, health or morals, or for the protection of the rights and freedoms of others.

The right to freedom of thought, conscience and religion underlies a pluralist society. It is a qualified right and it does not encompass a right to be free from criticism (see *Church of Scientology v Sweden* [1978]).

Permissible limitations

■ *Huber v Austria* [1971]: broad limitations on a prisoner's rights to practise religion, inherent in prison life, were accepted. In *X v Austria* [1965], the refusal to allow a Buddhist prisoner to grow a beard was not a violation.

■ *Arrowsmith v UK* [1978] recognised that Art 9 was not limited to 'conventional' religious beliefs and recognised that other beliefs and convictions may fall within the ambit of Art 9, in this case pacifism. Veganism has also been found to engage a persons rights under Art 9, *H v United Kingdom* [1993]. However this does not apply to every opinion or conviction held by an individual, see *Pretty v UK* [2002].

■ *R (SB) v Governors of Denbigh High School* [2006]: claimant was a Muslim schoolgirl who wished to wear a jilbab, contrary to school policy. HL held Art 9(1) was engaged but that the refusal to allow her to wear it was not, in the particular circumstances, an interference with her right to manifest her religious beliefs.

Article 10 – Freedom of expression

1 Everyone has the right to freedom of expression. This right shall include freedom to hold opinions and to receive and impart information and ideas without interference by public authority and regardless of frontiers. This article shall not prevent States from requiring the licensing of broadcasting, television or cinema enterprises.

2 The exercise of these freedoms, since it carries with it duties and responsibilities, may be subject to such formalities, conditions, restrictions or penalties as are prescribed by law and are necessary in a democratic society, in the interests of national security, territorial integrity or public safety, for the prevention of disorder or crime, for the protection of health or morals, for the protection of the reputation or rights of others, for preventing the disclosure of information received in confidence, or for maintaining the authority and impartiality of the judiciary.

Freedom of expression is considered fundamental to the Convention and as such Art 10 has been interpreted broadly and inclusively. As with Arts 8, 9 and 11, any interference must have a legitimate aim, must be prescribed by law and must be 'necessary' in a democratic society.

Injunctions against publication

■ *Sunday Times v UK* [1979]: the Attorney General in the UK had been granted an injunction against the publication of articles in the *Sunday Times* on the effects of thalidomide, pending a trial involving claims against the manufacturers of the drug. He claimed that the article would prejudice negotiations and amount to contempt of court. The ECtHR held that, given the length of time between publication and the trial, the restriction by way of an injunction was not necessary in the interests of society and consequently there was a violation of Art 10. The law on pre-trial publicity was subsequently changed in the UK.

■ *Handyside v UK* [1976]: a publication, *The Little Red Schoolbook*, was seized under the Obscene Publications Act 1959, despite the fact that it had been considered suitable for young people in a number of other European countries. The Court ruled that there was no violation of Art 10, as the 'protection of morals' clause in para (2) entitled the Government to impose restrictions that were proportionate. It was clear that the UK Government was given a considerable 'margin of appreciation' for what represented a moral danger.

- *Otto-Preminger Institut v Austria* [1994]: Austrian authorities had seized a satirical film, which depicted Jesus as mentally deformed, pending criminal proceedings. Again the ECtHR had found that the national authorities had not overstepped their margin of appreciation, particularly as Art 9 rights also fell to be protected. However, the Court did state that 'not only had the press the task of imparting information and ideas on political issues, the public had a right to receive them'.

- *Open Door Counselling and Dublin Well Woman v Ireland* [1992]: the Court ruled that an injunction preventing the dissemination of information on abortion and treatment advice was unlawful and contrary to Art 10.

- The question of whether expression of unpopular or offensive views should be protected depends on the motive of the person expressing or conveying them; eg, they may be justified in stimulating debate or giving an insight into the minds of racist organisations. *Jersild v Denmark* [1992] involved a conviction for a television programme that included interviews with a racist organisation. A breach of Art 10 was found by the Court.

- *Appleby and Others v UK* [2003]: the crucial point related to the forum for exercising freedom of expression. The applicants had been prevented from soliciting signatures for a petition in a town centre, which was in fact a shopping mall owned by a private company. As the mall was privately owned, the question was one of positive obligations. The Court did not exclude that a positive obligation to regulate property rights could arise but in the particular case it considered that the applicants had had available a variety of other ways in which to communicate their views to the public, for example by canvassing in the old town centre. Consequently, there had been no failure to protect the applicant's freedom of expression.

Article 11 – Freedom of assembly and association

1   Everyone has the right to freedom of peaceful assembly and to freedom of association with others, including the right to form and to join trade unions for the protection of his interests.

> 2   No restrictions shall be placed on the exercise of these rights other than such as are prescribed by law and are necessary in a democratic society in the interests of national security or public safety, for the prevention of disorder or crime, for the protection of health or morals or for the protection of the rights and freedoms of others. This article shall not prevent the imposition of lawful restrictions on the exercise of these rights by members of the armed forces, of the police or of the administration of the State.

The article grants a right to 'peaceful' assembly as opposed to assembly generally. A considerable 'margin of appreciation' has been given to States, including use of complete bans in order to prevent disorder (*Christians against Racism and Fascism v UK* [1995]).

The State has a complicated balancing act which must seek a compromise between the protection of individual freedoms, whilst maintaining order and protecting property. The HRA 1998 gave, for the first time, the UK Government an obligation to balance the exercise of restraints against rights.

As a brief summary of the law on the right to assemble in the UK, note that there was no right to assemble *per se* before HRA 1998. Law on the subject was generally provided by a series of statutes, imposed in response to various episodes of public disorder, for example, the Public Order Act 1936 was a response to the Fascist 'Blackshirt' marches of the time. In addition, the UK developed various common law powers which is now represented by the Police breach of the peace power of arrest.

UK Court Attitude
The attitude of the UK courts pre HRA 1998 may be seen as follows:

Duncan v Jones [1936]:

> 'English law does not recognise any special right of public meeting for political or other purposes. The right of assembly . . . is nothing more than a view taken by the court of the individual liberty of the subject.' Lord Hewitt CJ at 221.

DPP v Jones [1997]: 'The existence of a lawful excuse for doing something does not necessarily establish a legal right to do it.' Collins J.

However, on appeal to the House of Lords in *Jones v DPP* [1999] Lord Irvine LC said the law today is that the public highway is a public place which the public may enjoy for any reasonable purpose, provided the activity in question does not amount to a public or private nuisance and does not obstruct the highway by unreasonably impeding the primary right of the public to pass and repass: within these qualifications there is a public right of peaceful assembly on the highway.

(This updated the law from *Hirst v CC of West Yorkshire* [1986] 85 Cr App R 143 when the court held that only passing and repassing constituted a lawful use of the highway.) Whilst the HRA 1998 did not come into force for another year, it seems that the House of Lords in *Jones* were already taking it into account.

European Court Attitude

In Europe, the cases of *Platform Ärzre für das Leben v Austria* [1988], 13 EHRR 204 and *Ezelin v France* [1991] suggested a different interpretation of the right to assemble, the former suggesting that: 'A demonstration may annoy or give offence to persons opposed to the ideas or claims that it is seeking to promote. The participants must … be able to hold that demonstration without having to fear … such a fear would be liable to deter associations or other groups supporting common ideas or interests from openly expressing their opinions … In a democracy the right to counter-demonstrate cannot extend to inhibiting the exercise of the right to demonstrate.' And in the latter case: 'The Court considers … that the freedom to take part in a peaceful assembly – in this instance a demonstration that had not been prohibited – is of such importance that it cannot be restricted in any way … so long as the person concerned does not himself commit any reprehensible act on such an occasion.'

Union Membership

- *Young, James and Webster v UK* [1982], involving closed shop unions: the right to join a union was said to encompass a right not to join a union.

- *Council of Civil Service Unions v UK* [1985], otherwise known as the 'GCHQ case': a clear breach of Art 11 was found, but the ban from joining unions, for national security reasons, was justifiable under para (2) of the article.

UK Statute

Note that the UK has a number of restrictive Public Order Acts regulating the right to assemble, particularly in London, the major statutes being Public Order Acts

1936 & 1986, CJPOA 1994, Protection from Harassment Act 1997, Crime and Disorder Act 1998, Terrorism Act 2000, Anti Social Behaviour Act 2003 and Serious Organised Crime and Police Act 2005. Whilst these comply with Article 11, their use has been challenged in detail by the courts on a number of occasions.

Article 12 – Right to marry

Men and women of marriageable age have the right to marry and to found a family, according to the national laws governing the exercise of this right.

The protection afforded by Art 12 is relatively limited, particularly when seen in the context of changing attitudes to marriage and cohabitation. Generally, the Court will not interfere with national laws that regulate marriage. Article 12 does not encompass a right to divorce (*Johnston v Ireland* [1987]).

Transsexuals
- *Rees v UK* [1987] and *Cossey v UK* [1992]: the applicants argued that English law prevented them from entering a valid marriage. The Court, while expressing sympathy, found no breach of the Convention. However, more recently a different result was reached in *I v UK* [2002] and *Goodwin v UK* [2002] (see under Art 8 above).

Prisoners
- *Hamer v UK* [1981]: it was held that prisoners do have a right to marry, but restrictions inherent in the prison system are permissible so long as they do not affect the essence of the right.

- *X v UK* [1975]: the Court held that the denial of conjugal visits was not a violation of Art 12.

Article 13 – Right to an effective remedy

Everyone whose rights and freedoms as set forth in this Convention are violated shall have an effective remedy before a national authority notwithstanding that the violation has been committed by persons acting in an official capacity.

Although Art 13 has not been incorporated by the HRA 1998, the UK continues to be bound by the developing Strasbourg jurisprudence on the subject of effective remedies. Judicial review procedure, for example, is likely to continue to be challenged at Strasbourg, where it has been found wanting under Art 13 on several occasions. For challenges to judicial review as an effective remedy, see: *Chahal v UK* [1997]; *Smith and Grady v UK* [2000]; *Duyonov, Mirza, Sprygin, Ivanov v UK* [2000]; *Hatton and Others v UK* [2001]; and *HL v UK* [2004]. There have also been challenges under this article to the legal aid system as a denial of an effective remedy (see *McShane v UK* [2002]).

Judicial review: an effective remedy?

■ *Smith and Grady v UK* [2002]: the Court said of the concept of 'Wednesbury unreasonableness' that:

> ... the threshold at which ... the Court of Appeal could find the Ministry of Defence policy irrational was placed so high that it effectively excluded any consideration by the domestic courts of the question whether the interference with the applicant's rights answered a pressing social need or was proportionate to the national security and public order aims pursued ...

The adoption of the doctrine of proportionality into judicial review is likely to address this concern in part, but there remains the problem that judicial review is essentially a review of the procedures behind a decision; it provides no appeal against the merits of a decision. (See more on this in Chapter 5.)

Article 14 – Prohibition of discrimination

The enjoyment of the rights and freedoms set forth in this Convention shall be secured without discrimination on any ground such as sex, race, colour, language, religion, political or other opinion, national or social origin, association with a national minority, property, birth or other status.

Article 14 provides for a right not to be discriminated against, but only in respect of the other rights laid down in the Convention and its protocols. It is not a free standing prohibition on discrimination and does not apply unless the facts raise an issue of breach of another Convention right. However, the ECtHR has frequently found violations of Art 14 read in conjunction with another article of the Convention, without finding a violation of the latter. The principle is set out in *Grandrath v FRG* [1967].

Immigration

- *Abdulaziz and Others v UK* [1985]: female applicants wanted to bring their non-national spouses into the country, but were rejected. The Court found no violation of Art 8 but did find a violation of Art 14, since less stringent rules applied to husbands bringing in their spouses. The law was subsequently equalised.

- *Belgian Linguistic Case* [1968], the Court held that the principle of equality is violated if there is no objective or reasonable justification.

Article 15 – Derogation in time of emergency

1 In time of war or other public emergency threatening the life of the nation any High Contracting Party may take measures derogating from its obligations under this Convention to the extent strictly required by the exigencies of the situation, provided that such measures are not inconsistent with its other obligations under international law.

2 No derogation from Article 2, except in respect of deaths resulting from lawful acts of war, or from Articles 3, 4 (paragraph 1) and 7 shall be made under this provision.

3 Any High Contracting Party availing itself of this right of derogation shall keep the Secretary General of the Council of Europe fully informed of the measures which it has taken and the reasons therefor. It shall also inform the Secretary General of the Council of Europe when such measures have ceased to operate and the provisions of the Convention are again being fully executed.

Challenges to the validity of a derogation usually question the State's assertion that the situation prevailing is a 'time of war or other public emergency threatening the life of the nation.'

Challenges

A challenge to the UK's derogation from Art 5(3) (now withdrawn) on the basis that the situation prevailing in Northern Ireland did not amount to a public emergency was unsuccessful in *Brannigan and McBride v UK* [1993]. A wide 'margin of appreciation' was allowed to the UK.

The courts' approach

- *Lawless v Ireland (No 3)* [1961]: it was stated that a derogation is to be interpreted narrowly, being permitted only to the 'extent required by the exigencies of the situation'. In circumstances other than war, Art 15 requires either a crisis situation or an exceptional and imminent danger that 'affects the whole population and constitutes a threat to the organised life of the community of which the State is composed'.

Article 16 – Restrictions on political activity of aliens

Nothing in Articles 10, 11 and 14 shall be regarded as preventing the High Contracting Parties from imposing restrictions on the political activity of aliens.

Article 16 has been severely criticised as not being in the spirit of the ECHR, in that it is discriminatory and unnecessary. It implies that the freedoms of expression, association or assembly of an alien, as far as they involve political activities, can be restricted to an extent over and above the normal restrictions imposed in the second paragraph of the relevant articles.

Article 17 – Prohibition of abuse of rights

Nothing in this Convention may be interpreted as implying for any State, group or person any right to engage in any activity or perform any act aimed at the destruction of any of the rights and freedoms set forth herein or at their limitation to a greater extent than is provided for in the Convention.

Article 18 – Limitation on use of restrictions on rights

The restrictions permitted under this Convention to the said rights and freedoms shall not be applied for any purpose other than those for which they have been prescribed.

Articles 17 and 18 provide standard limitations to the interpretation of the Convention. It cannot be construed to abuse rights that should be protected, nor can the permissible restrictions be expanded upon.

Further substantive rights under various protocols

In addition, there are substantive rights contained in the protocols to the Convention. These are the right to peaceful enjoyment of possessions (First Protocol, Art 1), education (First Protocol, Art 2), right to free elections (First Protocol, Art 3), freedom of movement (Fourth Protocol, Art 2), abolition of the death penalty in peace time (Sixth Protocol), the right of appeal in criminal matters and compensation for wrongful conviction (Seventh Protocol, Arts 2 and 3), equality between spouses (Seventh Protocol, Art 5), freestanding right to non-discrimination (Twelfth Protocol) and abolition of the death penalty in time of war (Thirteenth Protocol). The UK has yet to ratify the Fourth, Seventh and Twelfth Protocols. In relation to the right to education (First Protocol, Art 2), the Government has entered a reservation such that the right is limited by the requirements of the Education Acts.

Hirst v UK [2004]: the Court found that the blanket disenfranchisement of convicted prisoners was incompatible with the right to vote.

You should now be confident that you would be able to tick all of the boxes on the checklist at the beginning of this chapter. To check your knowledge of The European Convention on Human Rights why not visit the companion website and take the Multiple Choice Question test. Check your understanding of the terms and vocabulary used in this chapter with the flashcard glossary.

Bringing rights home

3

The Human Rights Act 1998 is the culmination of a long campaign for the incorporation into domestic law of the European Convention on Human Rights.

Applauded in the House of Lords as 'a masterly exposition of the draftsman's art', the Act is generally regarded as providing an ingenious solution to the problem of protecting fundamental rights while maintaining parliamentary sovereignty. However, the radical changes in UK law produced by the Act should not be underestimated. In his article 'The Human Rights Act and parliamentary democracy' (1999) 62 *Modern Law Review*, KD Ewing asserts: 'It is unquestionably the most significant formal redistribution of political power in this country since 1911 and perhaps since 1688 ...'

BACKGROUND TO INCORPORATION OF THE ECHR

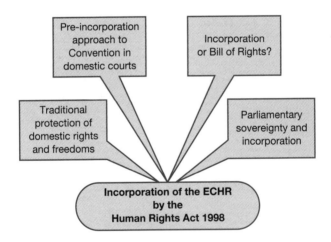

The Act came into force on 1 October 2000; ten years on from then, its importance and the extent to which it permeates the daily practice of lawyers is unparalleled. It is essential for any law student to have a clear grasp of the Act. This chapter traces the route to incorporation of the European Convention on Human Rights (ECHR) into English law.

THE TRADITIONAL APPROACH TO PROTECTING RIGHTS IN THE UK: 'RESIDUAL LIBERTIES'

In most constitutions there are declarations of particular rights or liberties to be accorded to citizens. Often these rights have an entrenched or protected status so that they cannot be temporarily restricted or overridden by the political majority of the day. The position in the UK has always been very much different. As AV Dicey famously expressed it:

> [In English law] the rules, which in foreign countries naturally form part of a constitutional code, are not the source but the consequence of the rights of individuals, as defined and enforced by the courts.
>
> (*An Introduction to the Study of the Law of the Constitution* (1885))

In other words, rights and freedoms were always regarded negatively in the UK; you could do anything you wanted provided there was no law against it, and equally you could be assured that your individual rights were protected unless an existing law explicitly gave permission to interfere with them. The law in question was the 'ordinary law enforced by the ordinary courts of the land'.

In *Entick v Carrington* [1765], a cornerstone case of civil liberties in the UK and the framework for the Fourth Amendment to the US Constitution, Entick, a critic of the King, had his house raided and personal papers taken by the authorities under a 'general' warrant. Entick sued on the basis that the warrant was unlawful. The House of Lords ruled in his favour, with Lord Camden making it clear that government, if it intends to interfere with individual rights, will need to point to specific statutory or common law powers. Similarly, the historic law of habeas corpus does not positively protect a right to liberty, but instead defines a remedy (namely an action for false imprisonment) where such liberty is lost.

According to Dicey, the absence of a written constitution in the UK is a strength, not a weakness. His thesis depended on the view that laws would only ever impose narrow and tightly defined areas of liability and that the judiciary would construe rules strictly against the executive. Any such laws would be created by a sovereign Parliament acting with a democratic mandate. The law would be precise, in as much as it flowed from specific judicial decisions giving specific remedies for infringement, rather than dependent on a vaguely worded constitutional document.

The system may appear weak, and indeed mystifying, to many who see a constitutional bill of rights as the cornerstone of liberty. However, a bill of rights is not an automatic guarantee of rights; its efficacy depends on the integrity of the institutions that apply it.

As Dicey pointed out, many freedoms, such as the freedom of the press, were maintained with much more alacrity in the UK during the 19th century than, say, in France, whose Constitution of 1791 proclaims freedom of expression and the liberty of the press, and yet whose great writers were often published abroad due to restrictive press laws enacted in France after the revolution.

Yet Dicey's thesis becomes less convincing in contemporary UK law. There has been much legislation that is not tightly or narrowly drawn in areas that may encroach upon civil liberties. Examples include the Criminal Justice and Public Order Act 1994, the Anti-Terrorism, Crime and Security Act 2001 and, most recently, the Prevention of Terrorism Act 2005. Powers of search and seizure, and even house arrest, under current legislation might leave a contemporary Mr Entick with much to fear. The view that judges will be robust in challenging the executive is also questionable given the considerable amount of deference that has been shown, for example, in relation to the use of prerogative powers by the executive. Furthermore, Dicey's paradigm of 'parliamentary sovereignty', with an all-pervasive Parliament continually adapting and adding to existing rights and remedies under the mandate of 'ordinary' Britons, is clearly under attack from the growth of executive power.

One further argument that is raised against the traditional approach is that even where a democratically elected Parliament is effective in translating the will of its electorate, democracy does not guarantee civil liberties. The policies that are adopted may reflect the populist majority view, while the rights of minorities are overlooked. This has raised particular concern recently where broad anti-immigration policies have gained popular support across Europe. As it was put in *The Three Pillars of Freedom; Political Rights and Freedoms in the United Kingdom* by Klug, Starmer and Weir (1995):

> ... not only are human rights best protected in a political system based on the 'will of the people'; but for that will to be freely debated and expressed in ways which give everyone the chance to be involved, certain fundamental rights must be protected. A majority decision is democratically legitimate only if it is a majority within a society of equals.

Therefore, dissatisfaction with the traditional method of protecting civil liberties was seen to grow in the 1990s, particularly since the long period of Conservative rule had seen many fundamental rights eroded under broad ranging legislation. Those who argued for giving fundamental rights a special status found encouragement in the increasingly 'Convention minded' decisions of some members of the judiciary in the years leading up to incorporation – although a clear and common understanding of what 'constitutional rights' meant and how they should be protected remained lacking in the British system.

THE ECHR IN THE BRITISH COURTS PRIOR TO INCORPORATION

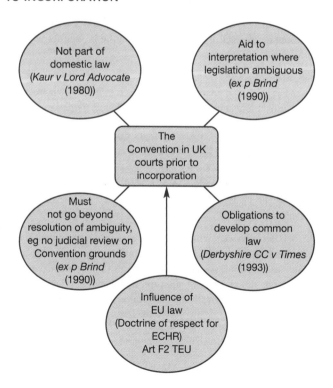

The approach of the UK courts towards the Convention has been the traditional dualist approach to international treaties, based on parliamentary sovereignty. They form no part of the domestic law until incorporated (see *Kaur v Lord Advocate* [1980]). Thus, in *Malone v Metropolitan Police Commissioner* [1979], despite expressing the view that the safeguards available against the 'unbridled' use of telephone tapping fell 'far short' of Convention principles, Sir Robert Megarry VC was nonetheless obliged to state:

> All that I do is to hold that the Convention does not, as a matter of English law, confer any direct rights on the plaintiff that he can enforce in the English courts.

Further confirming the principle of parliamentary sovereignty in *Re M and H (Minors)* [1983], Lord Brandon stated:

> English courts ... are bound to give effect to statutes which are free from ambiguity even if those statutes may be in conflict with the Convention.

However, where an ambiguity arose in legislation for the court to interpret, the ECHR could be used as an aid to establish Parliament's intention, but again that would not extend to a jurisdiction to enforce rights and freedoms under the Convention. Lord Bridge clarified the position in *R v Secretary of State for the Home Department ex p Brind* [1990]. The Home Secretary had used his discretionary power under s 29(3) of the Broadcasting Act 1981 to issue directives preventing broadcasters using the actual voices of members of certain proscribed organisations. The directives were challenged on the basis that they breached Art 10 rights. First, Lord Bridge enunciated the basic law of interpretation:

> But it is already well settled that, in construing any provision in domestic legislation which is ambiguous in the sense that it is capable of a meaning which either conforms to or conflicts with the Convention, the courts will presume that Parliament intended to legislate in conformity with the Convention, not in conflict with it.

Yet he went on to state that the Home Secretary was acting under legislation which was not ambiguous: he was acting within a discretion clearly given by the legislation. It was not for the court to go on and require the Home Secretary to use his discretionary powers in conformity with the ECHR, since that 'would be to go far beyond the resolution of an ambiguity [and] would be a judicial usurpation of the legislative function'.

The *Brind* decision was also illustrative of the regard to be had for the Convention in judicial review. The courts generally have shown reluctance to abandon the Wednesbury test, traditional in English public law, which assesses the reasonableness of an executive or administrative decision. There has been reluctance to adopt any test of 'proportionality', and in *Brind*, the court was unwilling to consider whether the minister could have taken a more 'Convention compliant' decision – although in other cases the courts did indicate that they would apply a more stringent test of reasonableness where fundamental rights were in play. In *Ministry of Defence ex p Smith* [1996], the court stated:

> The more substantial the interference with human rights, the more the court will require by way of justification before it will be satisfied that the decision was reasonable.

Outside of judicial review, the judges have felt less restrained in adopting ECHR principles in the development of the common law. They were free to employ the 'legal deceit' that the common law had always recognised the values contained in the Convention. The courts showed greatest resolve in relation to protecting 'freedom of expression' rights. In *Derbyshire CC v Times Newspapers* [1993] regarding the question of whether a local council could bring an action in libel against a newspaper, Butler-Sloss LJ in the Court of Appeal stated:

> Where there is ambiguity, or the law is otherwise unclear as so far declared by an appellate court, the English Court is not only entitled, but . . . obliged to consider the application of Article 10.

Similarly, Lord Goff in *AG v Guardian Newspapers (No 2)* [1990] considered it his duty, where free to do so, to interpret the law in accordance with the Convention.

The approach was not consistent, though. In relation to other Convention rights the courts adopted a less generous approach, particularly in dealing with matters such as protests and public order. As Lord Bingham pointed out in a lecture, 'The European Convention on Human Rights: time to incorporate' (*Law Quarterly Review*, 1993):

If in truth the common law as it stands were giving the rights of UK citizens the same protection as the Convention – across the board, not only in relation to Article 10 – one might wonder why the UK's record as a Strasbourg litigant was not more favourable.

THE IMPACT OF EU LAW

The UK's membership of the European Union (EU) should not be disregarded in relation to its importation of rights into the domestic courts. EU law mainly creates social and economic benefits. However, subsequent to the Amsterdam Treaty 1997, the EU has adopted a doctrine of respect for fundamental rights as outlined in the ECHR, which brings their consideration into the remit of the European Court of Justice. The full impact of this is not yet clear, but the EU has already had an important impact on domestic rights in providing sex discrimination, data protection and freedom of movement directives. EU law can, of course, have direct effect in UK courts and can override a UK statute (*Factortame* (1991)). As Lord Slynn noted, the effect of the recognition in EU law of Convention principles was that the Convention was entering by the 'back door'. Clearly, his implication was that the Convention should enter through the 'front door' via incorporation. It was, he said,

> ... quite plain that many, although perhaps not all, of the cases (going to Strasbourg) could be dealt with just as well and more expeditiously by our own judges here.
>
> (*House of Lords Debates*, 26 November 1992)

The separate impact of the EU Charter of Fundamental Rights (which contains rights similar to the ECHR with a number of additional social and worker rights) remains unclear. The new EU Constitution incorporated the Charter such that it would be made binding in the application of union law. However, it now seems unlikely that the Constitution will be ratified in its current form.

THE NEED FOR A 'HIGHER LAW'

In the years leading up to incorporation, it was clear that throughout the domestic legal system there was an increasing willingness to have consideration for fundamental rights. The inconsistencies and lack of definition in the traditional approach had highlighted the need to give such rights clear definition and status within domestic law. As Klug, Starmer and Weir (see p 56) put it:

> The three pillars of the 'British system' for protecting rights – Parliament, public opinion and the courts – requires the additional support of a consistent set of positive rights which act as a 'higher law', to which all legislation and policy must conform ... Such a resource would strengthen Parliament against the executive, would provide an additional support to public opinion, and would give the courts constitutional legitimacy and established standards and tests for the interpretation of statute, judicial review and the development of the common law.

Similarly, Lord Bingham expressed the judiciary's lack of power to protect fundamental rights in the absence of a 'higher' law:

> The elective dictatorship of the majority means that, by and large, the government of the day can get its way, even if its majority is small. If its programme or its practice involves some derogation from human rights Parliament cannot be relied on to correct this. Nor can judges. If the derogation springs from statute, they must faithfully apply the statute. If it is a result of administrative practice, there may well be no basis upon which they can interfere. There is no higher law, no frame of reference, to which they can properly appeal.
>
> ('The European Convention on Human Rights: time to incorporate' (*LQR*, 1993))

So the arguments were built for adopting a 'higher' law to protect fundamental rights. But what should the substance of the rights be? Most argued, as did Lord Bingham, for incorporation of the ECHR. But there were also those who argued that incorporation of the ECHR would not be enough, and that what was needed was a new domestic bill of rights, adapting and modernising Convention principles to the UK's own situation.

ARGUMENTS FOR A BILL OF RIGHTS

Those who argued for a domestic bill of rights were for the most part not arguing against incorporation. John Wadham agreed that incorporation was necessary as a 'first step' and that the ECHR should 'remain available to buttress a domestic Bill of Rights'. However, in *Why Incorporation of the ECHR is Not Enough* (1996) he examined the deficiencies of the Convention.

■ *Advantages of incorporation of the ECHR:*

- ready to hand;
- avoids protracted legislating;
- UK already bound internationally;
- rich body of Strasbourg jurisprudence;
- uniform development in European human rights.

■ *Disadvantages of incorporation of ECHR:*

- age of Convention;
- wide ranging exceptions;
- missing rights;
- difficulties in amending ECHR.

Wadham argues that in order to protect rights, at times the meaning of the text of the Convention has had to be stretched to a point of distortion, and in effect to judicial legislating. He uses the example of Art 8 providing adult gay men with protection from prosecution for consenting sexual intercourse (*Dudgeon v UK* [1981]), an interpretation that would not have occurred to those who drafted the ECHR. A new bill of rights could provide a much more comprehensible right to sexual privacy. He also points out a number of anachronisms in the Convention, including the right to imprison vagrants, alcoholics and those likely to spread infectious diseases under Art 5(1)(c). There is also the criticism that the Convention contains long lists of exceptions primarily tailored to the interests of State institutions.

The absence of certain rights from the Convention has also been highlighted – eg, the limited rights for asylum seekers and immigrants, lack of equality rights between spouses, limited anti-discrimination provisions and limited privacy rights.

Much debated was the absence of a 'right to know'. Article 10 (freedom of expression) might be relied upon to ensure that information obtained by journalists and others about government policies or misuses of power can be communicated to the public at large, but what of the information the Government decides should not be made available? The Convention provides no express right to obtain information. The importance of access to information was underlined by Ronald Dworkin, who observed:

> There is no genuine democracy . . . unless voters have had access to the information they need so that their votes can be knowledgeable rather than merely manipulated responses to advertising campaigns.
> (*Does Britain Need a Bill of Rights?* (1996))

Therefore, public scrutiny both of policy formulation and of the basis of decision taking is central to securing civil liberties and ensuring that a 'rights based culture' develops within government itself. Partially in response to these arguments and in order to supplement the HRA 1998, the Labour Government did introduce the Freedom of Information Act (FOIA) 2000, which came fully into force on 1 January 2005. This is a positive development from the previous position where there was no legal basis to obtain information, but the FOIA 2000 is severely limited, particularly in the area of access to government information, which is heavily guarded by class exemptions and a ministerial veto.

As regards the other missing rights, it might be argued that they can and have been addressed by means of additional protocols to the Convention. But this raises the further argument voiced by John Wadham for a domestic bill of rights: the procedural difficulties relating to the Convention. To amend or extend the Convention there are several procedural obstacles, 'not least of course the need to obtain the consent of more than 44 countries that are now members of the Council of Europe'. He contrasts this with a domestic bill of rights, which would provide a modern platform upon which Parliament would be free to develop rights.

ARGUMENTS AGAINST A BILL OF RIGHTS

Despite these deficiencies, the overwhelming majority of human rights bills considered by Parliament simply advocated the incorporation of the ECHR. The arguments against drafting a tailor-made domestic bill of rights centred on the fact that it would be an extremely burdensome task, involving an inordinate amount of the legislature's time. The difficulty of reaching cross-party agreement on the extent of rights was likely to result in unsatisfactory compromise. There was also the concern that the development of uniform European standards of human rights would be hindered. By contrast, the Convention was ready to hand with a long history of jurisprudence, and it was already binding on the UK internationally. Finally, the issue of missing rights could be dealt with by supplementary domestic legislation, such as the FOIA 2000, or by ratification of additional protocols to the Convention.

HOW COULD THE CONVENTION BE INCORPORATED?

Once the path to incorporation of the ECHR had been settled upon, the debate centred upon how this might be best achieved. How could Convention rights in the ECHR be 'entrenched' while at the same time maintaining the tradition of parliamentary sovereignty? The two questions asked were:

1 What is to stop outright repeal by a future Parliament of the entire Act incorporating the ECHR?
2 What will prevent inconsistent legislation overriding incorporated rights?

The first question regarding outright repeal was dealt with speedily by Lord Bingham:

> Constitutional experts point out . . . that the unwritten British constitution has no means of entrenching . . . a law of this kind. Therefore, it is said, what one sovereign Parliament enacts another sovereign Parliament may override: thus a government minded to undermine human rights could revoke the incorporation . . . I would give this argument beta for ingenuity and gamma, or perhaps omega, for political nous. It is true in theory that any Act of Parliament may be repealed. Thus theoretically the legislation extending the vote to the adult population, or giving the vote to women, . . . or safeguarding the independence of judges, or providing for adhesion to the European Community, could be revoked at the whim of a temporary majority. But absent something approaching a revolution in our society such repeal would be unthinkable.
>
> ('The European Convention on Human Rights: time to incorporate' (*LQR*, 1993))

The second question of dealing with 'inconsistent' legislation was of more practical concern to the Government. Should a power be given to the courts to strike down 'inconsistent' legislation? Could this be squared with parliamentary sovereignty? It is useful here to consider some models of 'entrenchment' or protection for certain laws (see the table at the end of the chapter for a summary of these models).

Initially rejected options

Two methods of entrenching or giving special status to a bill of rights used in other countries, particularly those with a written constitution, were dismissed at the outset as unworkable within the British constitution and the concept of parliamentary sovereignty:

1 *Full entrenchment*, such that the substance of certain laws can never be changed (eg, parts of German law are entrenched in this manner and they can never be repealed or amended unless there is a complete break with the existing legal order in Germany).

2 *Partial entrenchment*, which limits the 'manner' in which certain laws can be changed by future parliaments (eg, the US Constitution can only be amended by a proposal approved by two-thirds of each House of Congress, and such a proposal must then be ratified by three-quarters of the states' legislatures).

The argument that a sovereign British parliament cannot entrench laws by divesting itself of authority in these two ways is by no means settled among academics, but in any event these options were rejected as too controversial by the Labour Government in the White Paper, *Rights Brought Home: The Human Rights Bill*, introduced shortly after it came to power in 1997.

There remained, however, other weaker models of protection which afford special status to certain laws while maintaining parliamentary sovereignty. These were considered by the Government in the 1997 White Paper.

The models considered

1 European Communities Act (ECA) 1972, affording special status to EU law.

2 Existing models for protecting Bills of Rights in Commonwealth countries which maintained traditions of parliamentary sovereignty.

The European Communities Act 1972

Section 2(4) of this Act provides: 'any enactment passed or to be passed ... shall be construed and have effect subject to the foregoing provisions of this section.'

The 'foregoing provisions' are those in s 2(1) giving effect in the UK to directly effective EU law. In other words, directly effective EU law takes precedence over a domestic statute. Therefore, controversially, where a statute is in conflict with EU law, the inconsistent provisions of that statute must be set aside by the court (*Secretary of State for Transport ex p Factortame* (1989)). The concept of parliamentary sovereignty is said to remain undisturbed since it is available to Parliament to repeal the ECA 1972 outright and that, in disapplying the inconsistent provisions, the court is simply fulfilling Parliament's intention under the ECA 1972 to legislate compatibly.

Given that repeal of the ECA 1972 is politically unlikely, EU law is in effect entrenched (political entrenchment). The difficulty in applying this approach to incorporation of the ECHR is that there is no equivalent concept of 'directly effective' ECHR law. Other models needed to be considered.

Commonwealth models

■ Strong incorporation: the Canadian Charter of Rights and Freedoms 1982 enables the courts to strike down any legislation which is inconsistent with the Charter, unless it contains an explicit statement that it is to apply 'notwithstanding' the provisions of the Charter. It is said that parliamentary sovereignty is maintained since the judiciary will only be striking down a statute on the mandate of the democratically elected parliament.

Where such legislation is struck down it may be re-enacted with a 'notwithstanding' clause. Most commentators would suggest that governments are politically unlikely to use this type of clause, in so far as it would be a confession that legislation breaches basic rights. Therefore, this would represent a relatively strong form of protection.

■ Weak incorporation: in the New Zealand Bill of Rights Act 1990 there is no power to strike down a statute. It is an 'interpretative' statute which requires past and future legislation to be interpreted consistently with the rights in the Act as far as is possible, but provides that the legislation still stands if that is impossible.

■ A hybrid: the Hong Kong Bill of Rights Ordinance 1991 combined the two approaches, with all previous legislation subordinated to the Ordinance, but applying the 'interpretative approach' to future legislation.

Chosen model

As can be seen in detail in Chapter 4, the Government decided not to include in the HRA 1998 any power to disapply or 'strike down' primary legislation. In dismissing the approach under the ECA 1972, the Government differentiated between the UK's 'absolute' obligations under EU law as opposed to those under the ECHR. Nor was the Canadian model adopted, which also allows inconsistent statutes to be struck down. In the view of the White Paper, 'the Human Rights Bill is intended to provide a new basis for judicial interpretation of all legislation, not a basis for striking down any part of it'.

The approach chosen bore most similarity to the New Zealand model in being an 'interpretative only' statute. Section 3 of the HRA 1998 provides a 'rule of construction' to apply to past as well as future legislation, very similar to the New Zealand approach. Section 3 reads:

(1) So far as it is possible to do so, primary legislation and subordinate legislation must be read and given effect in a way which is compatible with the Convention rights.

Importantly, there is also the additional power under s 4 to make a 'declaration of incompatibility'. This will not in any way disapply or strike down primary legislation, but remains a powerful tool to put Parliament on notice that, in the courts' view, the legislation breaches Convention principles. The full details of this and the other innovations of the HRA 1998 are examined in Chapter 4.

Models for incorporation of ECHR

See table overleaf.

The Human Rights Act 1998 employs the approach of 'weak' incorporation (New Zealand) with no power for courts to strike down inconsistent primary legislation, but with additional power to make a 'declaration of incompatibility'.

	Type of protection	Power for Court to 'strike down' legislation?	Status of 'protected law'	Examples
Full entrenchment	Substance	Yes	Can never be repealed or amended	German Basic Law
Partial entrenchment	Manner	Yes	Procedural requirements before repeal or amendment permissible, eg public referendum or approval by 75% of legislative assembly	US Constitution
Political entrenchment	Form (of words) and manner?	Yes	Overrides all past and future legislation until such time as enabling statute is repealed (repeal theoretically possible, politically unlikely)	EU law by virtue of ECA 1972
'Strong' incorporation	Form (of words)	Yes (unless 'notwithstanding clause')	Overrides incompatible past legislation but future legislation subject to 'interpretative obligation' only	Canadian Charter of Rights and Freedoms 1982
Hybrid 'strong/weak' incorporation	Form (of words)	Past: Yes Future: No	Overrides incompatible past legislation but future legislation subject to 'interpretative obligation' only	Hong Kong Bill of Rights Ordinance 1991
'Weak' incorporation	Form (of words)	No	'Interpretative obligation' only (ie interpretation consistent with Bill of Rights to be preferred to any other meaning)	New Zealand Bill of Rights Act 1990

← Weakening of protection

You should now be confident that you would be able to tick all of the boxes on the checklist at the beginning of this chapter. To check your knowledge of Bringing rights home why not visit the companion website and take the Multiple Choice Question test. Check your understanding of the terms and vocabulary used in this chapter with the flashcard glossary.

The Human Rights Act 1998

4

This chapter looks in detail at the British 'model' of incorporation of the European Convention on Human Rights (ECHR), as implemented by the Human Rights Act (HRA) 1998. The chapter begins with the basic principles underlying the Act and then moves onto the most important sections of the Act, using illustrations where relevant.

INTRODUCTION

As noted in Chapter 3, the chosen approach to incorporation under the HRA 1998 is closer to the New Zealand model than the Canadian model. The Act adopts an 'interpretative' only approach and consequently the courts are not empowered to strike down incompatible primary legislation. The Lord Chancellor indicated that the intention was to learn from the experience of others but not to be constrained by it and that a 'distinctively British approach for our British Parliament and British courts' was to be adopted. There are a number of novel features in the British approach. The Lord Chancellor summed up the British model of incorporation as follows:

> The [Act] is based on a number of principles. Legislation should be construed compatibly with the Convention as far as is possible. The sovereignty of Parliament should not be disturbed. Where the courts cannot reconcile the legislation with Convention rights, Parliament should be able to do so – and more quickly if appropriate, than by enacting primary legislation. Public authorities should comply with Convention rights or face the prospect of legal challenge. Remedies should be available for a breach of Convention rights by a public authority.
>
> (House of Lords, 5 February 1998)

Note the following 'novel' features of incorporation:

- declarations of incompatibility (s 4);

- functional definition of public authorities (s 6);

- applicable directly in the UK courts (s 7);

- inclusion of courts and tribunals as 'public authorities' (s 6(3));

- power to take remedial action (s 10);

- special provisions in relation to Arts 10 (freedom of expression) and 9 (freedom of thought, conscience and religion) (ss 12 and 13);

- statements of compatibility on the face of new legislation (s 19).

NEW LEGAL CHALLENGES

The effect of the Act is that new legal challenges may be mounted against public authorities for breach of Convention rights, as illustrated in the diagram below.

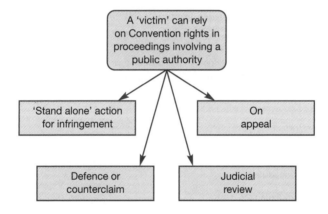

The normal position will be that where an applicant has had his or her Convention rights infringed by a public authority, any such action or omission will be unlawful, and consequently the applicant will be entitled to an appropriate remedy in the courts.

NO POWER TO DISAPPLY PRIMARY LEGISLATION

However, where an applicant has had his or her Convention rights infringed by a public authority, but the public authority was obliged to act in this manner by the provisions of primary legislation, the applicant will not be entitled to a remedy. This is because primary legislation cannot be struck down by the court and consequently the incompatible acts of the public authority remain valid and lawful. The court may make a 'declaration of incompatibility', but that will provide no remedy to the victim.

It may be that action is taken by the relevant minister or Parliament to remedy the offending legislation, but that will be of no assistance to the instant applicant, other than perhaps in ensuring that future actions of the public authority do not infringe Convention rights.

- *R (H) v Mental Health Review Tribunal* [2001]: the Review Tribunal, under provisions of the Mental Health Act (MHA) 1983, could only release a mental health patient from detention if they satisfied themselves that the patient was *not* suffering from mental disorder, rather than positively being satisfied he was so suffering. In effect this placed the onus of proof on the restricted person and as such could not be construed by the court as compatible with Art 5 of the ECHR, so a 'declaration of incompatibility' was made. The fact that the Tribunal was obliged to act incompatibly by primary legislation meant that their actions remained lawful and there was no successful cause of action for the applicant. However, this case generated the first remedial order under s 10 of the HRA 1998, and subsequent review of H's detention placed the burden of proof on the Tribunal.

OPERATION OF THE HRA 1998
See chart opposite.

Overview of the HRA 1998

Section 1	The Convention rights
Section 2	Interpretation of Convention rights

Legislation

Section 3	Interpretation of legislation
Section 4	Declaration of incompatibility
Section 5	Right of Crown to intervene

Public authorities

Section 6	Acts of public authorities
Section 7	Proceedings
Section 8	Judicial remedies
Section 9	Judicial acts

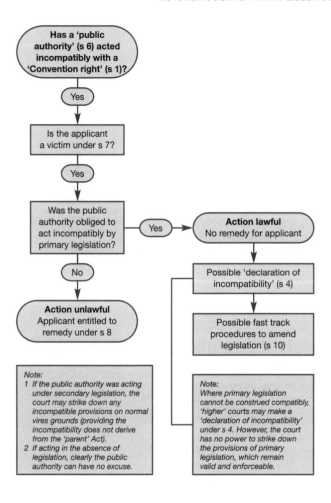

Has a 'public authority' (s 6) acted incompatibly with a 'Convention right' (s 1)?

Yes

Is the applicant a victim under s 7?

Yes

Was the public authority obliged to act incompatibly by primary legislation?

Yes → **Action lawful** No remedy for applicant

No

Action unlawful Applicant entitled to remedy under s 8

Possible 'declaration of incompatibility' (s 4)

Possible fast track procedures to amend legislation (s 10)

Note:
1 If the public authority was acting under secondary legislation, the court may strike down any incompatible provisions on normal vires grounds (providing the incompatibility does not derive from the 'parent' Act).
2 If acting in the absence of legislation, clearly the public authority can have no excuse.

Note:
Where primary legislation cannot be construed compatibly, 'higher' courts may make a 'declaration of incompatibility' under s 4. However, the court has no power to strike down the provisions of primary legislation, which remain valid and enforceable.

Remedial action

Other rights and proceedings

Derogations and reservations

Judges of the European Court of Human Rights

Parliamentary procedure

Schedules

DETAILED ANALYSIS OF THE ACT

For the rest of this chapter, the operation and impact of the important sections of the Act are examined in greater detail. The impact in recent case law is reviewed in Chapter 5.

The sections are not quoted here; to get the most out of this chapter, have a copy of the Act to hand (you can find this in a text and materials book, some statute books or at www.opsi.gov.uk/acts.htm).

SECTION 1: THE CONVENTION RIGHTS

As would be expected, the articles to be incorporated are those in the first section of the ECHR which contain the substantive rights. Procedural and other matters to be taken into account at Strasbourg are of no direct relevance domestically. However, note should be taken of the missing Arts 1 and 13. Article 1 provides that the State must secure to everyone the Convention rights contained in Section I of the ECHR; Art 13 provides that an effective remedy must be available to anyone whose Convention rights have been violated.

In relation to Art 1, the Government's view was that it was inappropriate to incorporate a general international obligation of this nature. The Lord Chancellor stated that the HRA 1998 as a whole 'gives effect to Article 1 by securing in the United Kingdom the rights and freedoms of the Convention'. In relation to Art 13, the Government took the view that s 8 of the HRA 1998 already provides exhaustive remedies 'and that nothing further is needed'. Yet the domestic courts may still have regard to Art 13 and its case law at Strasbourg when considering remedies under s 8, without being specifically bound by it.

SECTION 2: INTERPRETATION OF CONVENTION RIGHTS

The important point here is that Strasbourg jurisprudence does not bind domestic courts but they must take it into account. This would appear a logical position given that the UK is not bound in international law to follow the European Court of Human Rights (ECtHR) judgments in cases in which it was not the respondent. The Lord Chancellor amplified the position:

> [The Act] will of course permit UK courts to depart from existing Strasbourg decisions and upon occasion it might well be appropriate to do so and it is possible they might give a successful lead to Strasbourg.

As already noted in Chapter 3, Protocol 11 has restructured the approach at Strasbourg. The newly structured ECtHR is now the single adjudicative body there, and as such will be the sole source of future jurisprudence. However, the earlier decisions of the Commission and the Committee of Ministers under the old and now replaced Arts 26, 27, 31 and 46 need still to be considered.

SECTION 3: INTERPRETATION OF LEGISLATION

SECTION 4: DECLARATION OF INCOMPATIBILITY

Sections 3 and 4 are at the heart of the British model of incorporation. They need to be considered together as a package. Lord Irvine, the Lord Chancellor at the time of enactment, explained the interaction of the two sections in the House of Lords:

> The Bill sets out a scheme for giving effect to the Convention rights which maximises the protection to individuals while retaining the fundamental principle of parliamentary sovereignty. [Section] 3 is the central part of the scheme. Section 3(1) requires legislation to be read and given effect to so far as is possible to do so in a way that is compatible with Convention rights. Section 3(2) provides that where it is not possible to do so . . . that does not affect its validity, continuing operation or enforcement. This ensures the courts are not empowered to strike down Acts of Parliament which they find to be incompatible with Convention rights. Instead section 4 of the [Act] . . . introduces a new mechanism through which the courts can signal to the government that a provision of legislation is, in their view, incompatible. It is then for government and Parliament to consider what action should be taken.
>
> (House of Lords, Report stage of the Bill)

Section 3: Interpretation of legislation
'So far as it is possible to do so, . . .'

In explaining this rule of construction, the Lord Chancellor stated, 'we want the courts to construe statutes so that they bear a meaning that is consistent with the Convention whenever that is possible but not when it is impossible to achieve that' (House of Lords, 18 November 1997).

Comparison with previous approach to interpretation

As noted in the last chapter, previously the court was only enabled to take the Convention into account in resolving an ambiguity in a legislative provision. According to the Lord Chancellor, the new rule of construction:

> ... goes far beyond the [previous] rule. It will not be necessary to find an ambiguity. On the contrary the courts will be required to interpret legislation so as to uphold the Convention rights unless the legislation itself is so clearly incompatible with the Convention that it is impossible to do so.

Further, he approved the use of the same interpretative techniques as used to ensure domestic legislation complies with EC law, saying:

> ... even when this requires straining the meaning of words or reading in words which are not there.

> (Tom Sargant Memorial Lecture, 1998)

Examples of the courts' approach so far

In practice, the approach of the courts to applying new interpretative techniques has varied between what have been called 'activist' and 'minimalist' approaches. An example of the activist approach would be *R v A*; an example of the minimalist approach would be *Brown v Stott*.

- *R v A* [2001]: the House of Lords adopted an extremely creative interpretative approach by reading implied words into a legislative provision. The case concerned s 41(3)(c) of the Youth Justice and Criminal Evidence Act 1999, which in rape cases expressly prohibits evidence being adduced of a woman's previous sexual relations with the defendant. On the face of it, the provision seemed incompatible with the defendant's Art 6 right to a fair trial, in that such evidence could be crucial to establishing his belief as to her consent, and a declaration of incompatibility might have been made. However, the House of Lords avoided a declaration, which was referred to as a 'measure of last resort', and instead read into s 41(3)(c) an implied qualification that evidence that is necessary to ensure a fair trial under Art 6 should not be rendered inadmissible by the section, and therefore the evidence could be adduced in relation to consent. To use Lord Steyn's words, this was an interpretation 'which linguistically will appear strained'.

■ *Brown v Stott* [2001] exemplified the minimalist approach. In that case, the Law Lords had to rule on whether s 172 of the Road Traffic Act 1998 was compatible with the Art 6 right to a fair trial. The section makes it an offence for motorists not to tell the police who was driving their vehicle. The coerced statement can then be used as evidence at trial for the particular offence in question. The provision offended against the right to freedom from self-incrimination. The Lords ruled that the s 172 rule was not incompatible with Art 6 on the basis that the freedom from self-incrimination was not an absolute right and that the general interest of the community needed to be taken into account. The Lords also stated that deference should be shown to the legislature's 'discretionary area of judgment'.

Attorney-General's Reference (No 4) of 2002 considered whether s 11 of the Terrorism Act 2000 was incompatible with Art 6, and it was held that while imposing a legal burden on the defendant would be incompatible, s 11 could be read as to be imposing an **evidential** burden on the defendant which was not in violation of Art 6.

In *Bellinger v Bellinger* [2003] the House of Lords held that it was not possible to interpret the Matrimonial Clauses Act 1971 in such a way as to include a person who had undergone gender reassignment. However this can be contrasted with the decision in *Mendoza v Ghaidan* [2004] where the House of Lords interpreted the Rent Act 1977 which stated 'living together as man and wife' to include homosexual couples.

Limits of interpretation

(1) judicial legislating; (2) retrospectivity

The limits to powers of interpretation should be remembered. First, the court should have regard to the distinction to be made between legitimate interpretation and the redrafting of statutes. For example, in *Re W and B (Children: Care Plan)* [2002], the Court of Appeal interpreted provisions in the Children Act 1989 to include a duty on local authorities to be subject to 'starred milestones'; in other words, they were required to implement care plans within time limits. There was no such express provision in the legislation. The House of Lords ruled that this interpretation went beyond the boundaries of legitimate interpretation. Secondly, s 22(4) of the HRA 1998 puts express limits on the retrospective application of the Act.

Section 4: Declarations of incompatibility

The expected approach to the making of declarations was outlined by the Home Secretary in the Commons, where he stated: 'We expect that, in almost all cases, the court will be able to interpret legislation compatibly with the Convention. However, we need to provide for the rare cases where that cannot be done ...' This would seem to approve the approach in *R v A* above, where the court referred to a declaration as a 'measure of last resort'. Where a declaration of incompatibility is made under s 4, the Home Secretary continued, 'it is likely that the Government and Parliament would wish to respond to such a situation and would do so rapidly' (House of Commons, 3 June 1998).

Who can issue a declaration?
Under s 3(5), only specified higher courts can issue a declaration of incompatibility, including the High Court, the Court of Appeal and the House of Lords.

Not a remedy for the applicant
An anomaly arises in that an applicant may wish to argue that a declaration under s 4 should not be made. A declaration does not provide a remedy for an applicant, since incompatible legislation remains valid and consequently the public authority's incompatible acts remain lawful. If the court can be persuaded to construe the provisions of the legislation so that they bear a meaning that is consistent with the Convention, however strained, then it may be argued that the public authority acted unlawfully by not following that 'strained' interpretation.

■ *R (H) v Mental Health Review Tribunal* [2001]: the preferred submission of the applicant was not that provisions of the Mental Health Act (MHA) 1983 were incompatible with Art 5, which would require a declaration of incompatibility; that would leave the applicant with no cause of action against the public authority, which had faithfully followed primary legislation. Instead it was argued that the court could construe the legislation compatibly and in so doing it would find that the tribunal had not acted within this compatible interpretation. In the event, the court found that it was impossible to construe the legislation compatibly and a declaration was made, leaving the applicant without a remedy.

Subordinate legislation
Section 3(2)(c) creates a distinction between incompatible subordinate legislation where the parent Act prevents removal of the incompatibility,

and incompatible subordinate legislation where that is not the case. In the case of the former, the subordinate legislation remains valid since to hold otherwise would be to disregard a provision of primary legislation, though a declaration of incompatibility may be made under s 4(4). In the case of the latter, the subordinate legislation may be struck down on normal *ultra vires* grounds.

Declarations of incompatibility made by the courts
A list of declarations made under s 4 can be found at www.human rights. gov. uk.decihm/htm.

SECTION 5: RIGHT OF THE CROWN TO INTERVENE
The object of s 5 is to ensure that the appropriate minister, in the event of a declaration of incompatibility, is fully apprised of the court's view as to why a declaration is necessary.

It will also afford the minister the opportunity to address the court on the object and purpose of the allegedly offending legislation.

SECTION 6: ACTS OF PUBLIC AUTHORITIES
Section 6 was explained as follows by the Home Secretary:

'[Section] 6 makes it unlawful for public authorities to act in a way that is incompatible with a Convention, unless they are required to do so to give effect to primary legislation.'

'. . . any person certain of whose functions are functions of a public nature . . .'

Functions of a public nature
There are three categories of functions of a public nature, as illustrated opposite.

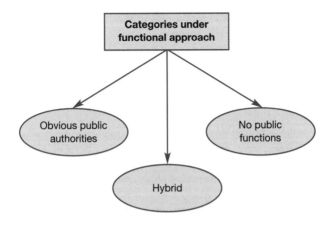

Bodies		Liability under HRA 1998
1	Obvious public authorities, all of whose functions are public (eg government departments, the police)	All acts subject to liability under the Act
2	Hybrid organisations with a mix of public and private functions (eg the BBC, security companies who run prisons)	Liable for their 'public' acts but not for 'private' acts (s 6(5))
3	Organisations with no public functions (eg the press)	No liability (subject to horizontal effect?)

The approach of the courts

The approach to defining public authorities has been variable and at times unexpectedly cautious.

▩ *R (Heather) v Leonard Cheshire Foundation* [2002]: the LCF, a private charity, provides accommodation for the disabled; some of its homes are funded by the local authority. The court held that residents of homes funded by the local authority could rely on their Convention rights against that authority, but controversially not against the charity, as it was held that it was not exercising public functions. Similarly, in *RSPCA v Meade* [2001] the RSPCA was not considered a 'public authority'.

Horizontal effect: liability under the HRA 1998?

The inclusion of courts and tribunals under s 6(3)(a) is of great importance and has been the focus of considerable academic debate. The main question posed was whether this would give a 'horizontal effect' to the Act, in other words, would the Act have effect in actions between private parties? The law is still developing but the position adopted so far by the courts may be explained as follows.

Section 6(1) plainly states that it is only the acts of public authorities that are subject to liability under the HRA 1998 (vertical effect). On the basis of the approach in s 6, clearly it cannot have been intended that the Act should confer directly enforceable rights between individuals. Therefore, there is no direct horizontal effect. However, the inclusion of courts and tribunals as public bodies under s 6(3)(a) requires them to act compatibly with Convention rights, and so, it is argued, this creates what has been called an 'indirect' horizontal effect. In other words, although the parties in private proceedings will not be able to rely on Convention rights directly, the courts have a duty to apply the law compatibly with Convention rights in those proceedings. That duty includes both interpreting legislation and developing the common law in line with the Convention, in effect giving the Act horizontal application.

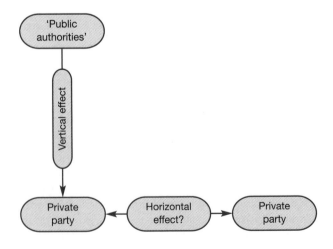

INDIRECT HORIZONTAL EFFECT

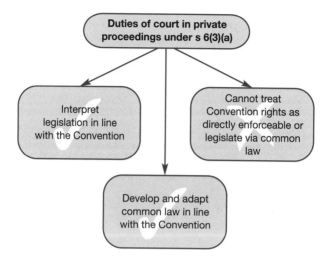

First, there will be an indirect horizontal effect where the court is required to interpret legislation affecting proceedings. Secondly, though less clear cut, there is the possibility of a horizontal effect by virtue of the court's duty to develop the common law in line with the Convention. The *Douglas* case (see below) suggests that the development of the common law will provide an indirect horizontal effect to the Act, at least in relation to some ECHR articles. In that case, Arts 8 and 10 were under consideration and therefore s 12 of the HRA 1998 fell to be interpreted. Note that *Douglas* was an interim application and not a trial, and therefore *obiter* as to the law, although the approach was confirmed in *Campbell v Mirror Group Newspapers Ltd* [2004].

▓ *Douglas v Hello!* [2001]: the marriage of Michael Douglas and Catherine Zeta Jones was photographed without permission and *Hello!* magazine intended to publish the photographs. The couple sought an interim injunction to restrain publication. The question that arose was whether the couple would be able to rely on a common law right to privacy arising out of Art 8 of the ECHR. Previously the common law had not recognised a right to privacy (*Kaye v Robertson* [1991]).

In considering the impact of the HRA 1998, Sedley LJ posed the question: does s 6(3)(a) simply require the court's procedures to be Convention-compliant or does it require the law applied by the court to give effect to Convention principles, even where proceedings are between private parties? He was unwilling to answer the question in respect of all Convention rights, but in relation to Art 8 rights Sedley LJ's view was that the impetus of the HRA 1998 was such that the existing common law doctrine of breach of confidence could be developed to protect privacy rights between private parties.

Lord Irvine expressed some words of caution in relation to the development of the common law, saying, 'the courts may not act as legislators and grant new remedies for infringement of Convention rights unless the common law itself enables them to develop new rights or remedies' (House of Lords, 24 November 1997).

SECTION 7: PROCEEDINGS

Section 7 governs standing and access to justice under the HRA 1998.

Standing: 'victim' test

Section 7(1) requires an applicant who brings a case under the HRA 1998 to be a 'victim'; this mirrors the approach at Strasbourg. The 'victim' test for standing is narrower than the 'sufficient interest' test used in judicial review proceedings, where public interest groups are allowed to bring cases on occasion. The domestic courts will be allowed to hear submissions (amicus briefs) from public interest groups under the Act but they will not be treated as full parties.

There has, though, been flexibility in applying the 'victim' test at Strasbourg, an approach which is likely to be adopted by the domestic courts. Applications have been allowed at Strasbourg where there is only a potential infringement of a victim's rights. There must be a reasonable likelihood that the applicant would be subject to the impugned (questioned) measure. Applications have also been allowed from indirect victims, such as relatives affected by the violation of an individual's rights.

- *Campbell and Cosans v UK* [1982]: children at a school where corporal punishment was practised were considered victims on the basis that they had a 'direct and immediate interest in complaining', even though they had not in fact been punished.

▨ *Sutherland v UK* [1998]: the applicant was a victim for the purposes of challenging the age of consent for lawful homosexual intercourse. This was despite the fact that he had never been prosecuted nor was likely to be.

▨ *McCann and Others v UK* [1995], otherwise known as the 'Death on the Rock' case: relatives were allowed to bring cases on behalf of IRA terrorists shot dead in Gibraltar.

Section 7(3) confirms that where an HRA claim is brought by way of judicial review, the narrower 'victim' test will apply.

Access to justice

Under s 7(5), proceedings must be brought against a public authority within one year; under s 7(5)(b), the court has a discretion to extend the period where equitable to do so. The rule is subject to any stricter time limits which may already exist, such as the three month time limit in relation to judicial review.

SECTION 8: JUDICIAL REMEDIES

Section 8 provides that where a court finds that a public authority has acted unlawfully in infringing an applicant's Convention rights, a court may grant 'whatever remedy is available to it and which seems just and appropriate' (House of Lords, 3 November 1997). Courts and tribunals will be limited to remedies that are within their statutory powers.

A remedy might include the award of damages, in which case under s 8(4) regard should be had to awards made at Strasbourg and the concept of 'just satisfaction' under Art 41 of the ECHR. This would suggest that awards are likely to be low.

Criminal proceedings

Under s 8(2), damages cannot be awarded in criminal proceedings. If during the course of a criminal trial it emerges that a violation of an individual's Convention rights has occurred, that individual will be required to pursue any matter of damages separately through the civil courts. However, the utility of the HRA 1998 for defendants in criminal trials is more likely to be seen in the requirements of a fair trial under Art 6 and the possible exclusion of evidence which has been collected unlawfully in breach of Convention rights. The appeal process will also provide a remedy for the defendant for breaches of Convention rights arising at trial.

SECTION 9: JUDICIAL ACTS

The purpose of s 9 is to preserve the principle that proceedings against a court or tribunal on Convention grounds can only be brought by way of judicial review or on appeal.

However, there is one exception. Sub-section (3) provides an exception to the general rule that awards of damages cannot be made in respect of incompatible judicial acts: this is where the applicant has been the victim of arrest or detention in contravention of Art 5 of the ECHR. Article 5(5) requires that a right to compensation be available in such cases. Such damages may therefore be the subject of proceedings outside the normal principle.

SECTION 10: POWER TO TAKE REMEDIAL ACTION

Section 10 is an important innovation of the HRA 1998 and provides fast track procedures to amending legislation either:

1   where a declaration of incompatibility has been made, or
2   in response to a finding of the ECtHR.

In normal circumstances, any amendment to legislation must be made by Parliament, but in some circumstances the Government will want to bring legislation into line with human rights requirements more quickly than the normal parliamentary process allows. In such case a remedial order to amend legislation (primary or secondary) may be made by a minister. It may only be made after the appeal process has been exhausted and there must be 'compelling reasons' to do so. Safeguards to the use of such an 'executive' power are that it may only be used to remove incompatible provisions of legislation and to protect human rights. Concerns about the lack of parliamentary scrutiny were addressed by additional procedural requirements in Sched 2 to the Act governing the use of the orders. The schedule requires a draft of the order to be laid before Parliament, including an explanation of the incompatibility and the reasons for proceeding under s 10. There are also minimum periods of consultation during which representation may be made. Significantly, in exceptionally urgent cases, para 2(b) of the schedule allows the minister to make the order prior to laying the draft before Parliament.

It is important to remember that where a declaration of incompatibility is made, there is no obligation on the minister or Parliament to amend the relevant legislation. As an example, a court might make a declaration after finding that abortion legislation is incompatible with Art 2 rights to life, but the Government would have no wish or obligation to amend the relevant legislation.

SECTION 11: SAFEGUARD FOR EXISTING HUMAN RIGHTS

Section 11 clarifies that Convention rights are the 'floor of rights' and allows other human rights jurisprudence in addition to Strasbourg's to be taken into account where appropriate. Section 11 also confirms that all existing methods for the protection of civil liberties developed under the common law remain available to the applicant.

SECTION 12: FREEDOM OF EXPRESSION

Sections 12 and 13 were the result of protracted debate during the Bill's passage through Parliament and, in particular, intense lobbying on behalf of the press and religious bodies.

Section 12 applies where the court is considering whether or not to grant an injunction that would restrict freedom of expression, eg, restricting a newspaper from publishing photographs that may violate an individual's Art 8 rights – as in *Douglas v Hello!* [2002].

In such circumstances, s 12(4) requires the court to have 'particular regard' to Art 10 rights, taking into account whether or not the material is already in the public domain, whether there are any public interest reasons for publishing, and having regard to any privacy code such as the Press Complaints Commission's code, which outlines standards of behaviour expected of the press.

The intention of the section is to support freedom of expression, for example in cases where Art 10 and Art 8 rights clash. However, the Home Secretary made it clear that the section does not give precedence to Art 10 rights. Indeed, in recent case law, having 'particular regard' for Art 10 has been interpreted by the courts to mean having 'equal regard' for Art 8. In *Douglas v Hello! Ltd* [2001], Sedley LJ stated the position as follows:

> ... by virtue of s 12(1) and (4) [of the 1998 Act] the qualifications set out in Art 10(2) are as relevant as the right set out in Art 10(1). This means, for example, the reputations and rights of others – not only but not least their Convention rights – are as material as the defendant's right of free expression. So is the prohibition on the use of one party's Convention rights to injure the Convention rights of others.

Consequently, the section has been used to support developments in the common law to protect Art 8 'privacy' rights – eg, where there are flagrant breaches of the Press Complaints Commission's code. See also *Thompson and Venables v News Group Newspapers and Others* [2001] where, when considering Art 10 rights, equal regard was had for Art 2 rights. The lives of the two boys who had killed Jamie Bulger would have been at risk had newspapers been allowed to publish their identities.

- *Campbell (Naomi) v Mirror Group Newspapers Ltd* [2004]: *The Mirror* published an article with photographs of C, a model, leaving Narcotics Anonymous meetings. The article asserted that C was a drug addict. C had previously denied that she was an addict. Following the guidance given by Lord Woolf CJ in *A v B* [2002], Morland J at first instance stated:

  > ... A public figure is entitled to a private life. The individual, however, should recognise that because of his public position he must expect and accept that his actions will be more closely scrutinised by the media.

  The judge awarded damages to C on the basis that the newspaper had been justified in uncovering her false denials but not in publishing the accompanying photographs. In order to meet the requirements of s 12 of the HRA 1998 the media should:

  > ... respect information about aspects or details of the private lives of celebrities and public figures which they legitimately choose to keep private ... unless there is an overriding public interest duty to publish.

  Following appeals, the judge's decision was upheld by the House of Lords.

SECTION 13: FREEDOM OF THOUGHT, CONSCIENCE AND RELIGION

Section 13 addressed concerns raised during the passage through Parliament that the HRA 1998 might interfere with religious practices in a number of ways.

Examples cited included concerns that the Act might force Catholic priests to marry divorced or homosexual couples, or oblige church schools to retain staff of different religious backgrounds. While the section does not provide absolute protection for churches or religious organisations, it nonetheless requires the court to pay 'particular regard' to rights guaranteed under Art 9 of the Convention, including the right of a church to act in accordance with religious belief.

SECTIONS 14–17, SCHED 3: DEROGATIONS AND RESERVATIONS

These sections incorporate derogations and reservations made by the UK in relation to the ECHR. They detail procedures relating to the addition or removal of derogations and reservations from Sched 3 and the periods of time for which they may have effect.

SECTION 19: STATEMENTS OF COMPATIBILITY

This section is one of the novel features of the Act and is potentially very important. Ministers are required to make a statement on the face of all new Bills regarding whether the provisions of new legislation are compatible with the Convention.

The requirement should have a significant impact on the scrutiny of draft legislation within government. In most cases it will be expected that legislation will be stated to be compatible. Where such a statement cannot be made, parliamentary scrutiny of the Bill is likely to be intense.

The interaction with s 3 (interpretation of legislation) should also be noted. The fact that the minister has declared the legislation to be compatible will give all the more impetus to the courts to interpret legislation purposively to protect Convention rights.

> You should now be confident that you would be able to tick all of the boxes on the checklist at the beginning of this chapter. To check your knowledge of The Human Rights Act 1998 why not visit the companion website and take the Multiple Choice Question test. Check your understanding of the terms and vocabulary used in this chapter with the flashcard glossary.

Recent developments

Concept of the ECHR being a 'living instrument'	
Approaches intepreting recent legislation	
Right to Life	
Right to Private and Family Life	
Freedom of the Press v Private Life	

Note – students should review and add to this list as the case law develops

In this chapter, recent developments in domestic case law are briefly digested in relation to the relevant European Convention of Human Rights (ECHR) articles. The chapter ends with an attempt to form some conclusions on the impact of the Human Rights Act (HRA) 1998 so far.

The chart below illustrates the primary issues since enactment of the HRA 1998.

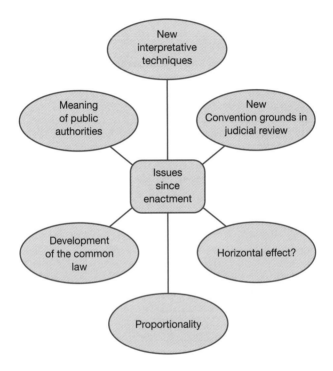

The more recent approaches of the UK towards the prevention of terrorism in response to events such as 9/11 and the London bombings highlight the impact of the incorporation into UK domestic law of the European Convention of Human Rights and the parallel approach to the interpretation of the European Court on Human Rights, whereby the concept of the convention as a living instrument has been earnestly pursued. This is shown by the fact that a court must assess the measures taken by the Government in the light of the oft used phrase what is 'necessary in a democratic society'. It is necessary to consider the particular circumstances in a particular time and place in order to make a judgment as to what the phrase actually means.

The case of *Chahal v UK* [1997] concerns attempts by the British Government to deport Mr Chahal back to India, on the grounds that his continued presence in the UK was not conductive to the public good, significantly in regard to potential terrorist activity. Mr Chahal claimed that he had been tortured by the India Police and was certainly involved to some degree with the movement for an independent Sikh State as the founder of the International Sikh Youth Federation. He was arrested after a meeting in Southall and subsequently claimed that if deported he would suffer inhuman and degrading treatment, contrary to Art 3 of the European Convention on Human Rights, at the hands of the Indian authorities. The Government argument was although this situation would indeed normally result in a violation of Art 3, this should not be relevant where the activities of the deportee may be considered as damaging to national security.

The Strasbourg Court rejected this argument, holding that, regardless of the nature of the particular activities of the individual it could never excuse a violation of Art 3, and that the non-derogable right should therefore still be inviolable, and that therefore even an unwanted and potentially dangerous individual should not be deported in circumstances concerning Art 3, a principle stemming from *Soering v UK* [1989]. The effect of this decision is that, in the absence of satisfactory assurance from the receiving State, even a dangerous terrorist could not be deported.

Further challenges to legislation passed regarding measures to attempt to prevent terrorism have arisen regarding Art 5.

- *A & Others v Secretary of State for the Home Department* [2004]: in perhaps the most important decision since incorporation, the House of Lords considered measures for indefinite detention contained in Part 4 of the Anti-terrorism, Crime and Security Act 2001. The provisions empowered the Home Secretary to detain indefinitely without charge or trial foreign nationals he suspected of links with international terrorism. The extended power of detention could not be justified under Art 5(1)(f) and therefore, in parallel to the enactment of the 2001 Act, the Government

95

entered a derogation to its obligations under Art 5(1). The detainees appealed on the basis that the derogating measures were unlawful because the requirements set out in Art 15(1) governing derogation were not satisfied. They submitted that (1) there was not a 'public emergency threatening the life of the nation'; (2) even if there was, the measures taken were not limited to those 'strictly required by the exigencies of the situation'; and furthermore, in a 'core' submission the detainees submitted that (3) the measures were discriminatory contrary to Art 14. The House of Lords held that the Government had been entitled to conclude that there was a public emergency. However, the derogating measures were disproportionate. The choice of an immigration measure to address a security problem had the inevitable result of failing adequately to address that problem (by allowing non-UK suspected terrorists to leave the country with impunity and leaving British suspected terrorists at large) while imposing the severe penalty of indefinite detention on persons who, even if reasonably suspected of having links with Al-Qaeda, may harbour no hostile intentions towards the United Kingdom. The measures were therefore not 'strictly required' by the exigencies of the situation within Art 15. Furthermore, the measures discriminated contrary to Art 14. It was not disputed that the relevant threat that the measures sought to address emanates both from UK and foreign nationals. Therefore, for the measures to be solely directed at non-nationals must be discriminatory. There can be no objective justification for the discrimination given the source of the threat has nothing to do with nationality. Therefore, there was a violation of Art 14. The court quashed the Human Rights Act 1998 (Designated Derogation) Order 2001 (as subordinate legislation) and consequently granted a declaration under s 4 of the HRA 1998 that Part 4 of the 2001 Act was incompatible with Arts 5 and 14. The Government has since repealed the measures and the derogation has been withdrawn.

PREVENTION OF TERRORISM ACT 2005

Under s 2(1) Prevention of Terrorism Act 2005, control orders can be imposed on a terrorist suspect if the UK has 'reasonable grounds for suspecting that the individual is or has been involved in terrorism-related activity' and it is considered necessary to make the order for the purposes connected with protecting the public from the threat of terrorism.

The conditions which accompany the order are varied, but usually include electronic tagging, the surrender of passport, limitations on the area where one might travel, usually combined with a curfew and regular reporting to the police, and limits on association with people (who themselves may be subject to police checks) and limitations on communications.

These orders have, from the start, aroused a great deal of controversy, and have led to a number of judicial challenges based on Article 5 of the ECHR, the right to liberty and security, and Art 6 ECHR, the right to a fair trial, for example *Secretary of State for the Home Department v JJ and others* [2006], *Secretary of State for the Home Department v MB* [2006] and *Secretary of State for the Home Department v E* [2007].

Clash with Art 8 rights

There have been important developments in the common law in cases where individuals have sought to rely on the HRA 1998 to protect their privacy from press intrusions. While the courts have been reluctant to state that a new right to privacy has emerged nonetheless the HRA has given considerable impetus to developing the law in this direction. The case law also provides examples of the 'indirect' horizontal application of the Act in disputes between private parties.

■ *Douglas v Hello!* [2001–2005]: in the light of the HRA 1998 the court was willing to consider the extension of the common law to protect privacy rights. The court considered s 12 of the HRA 1998. The phrase in s 12(4) to 'have particular regard' for ECHR Art 10 rights was taken to mean having *equal* regard for the limitations to the right contained in the second paragraph of the ECHR Article, which included 'the rights and reputations of others', in other words the court must have equal regard for Art 8 rights. This was the impetus to developing the common law to include a novel respect for privacy rights. This approach was subsequently confirmed by the House of Lords.

■ *Campbell v Mirror Group Newspapers Ltd* [2004]: M had published stories about C relating to her attendance at Narcotics Anonymous meetings. C had previously stated publicly that she did not take drugs. The House of Lords held that the publication of the fact that C was seeking treatment was necessary to set the record straight given her previous statements, but the additional information, including the photographs, was an unjustified intrusion into C's private life. Balancing the competing interests, C's right to

97

privacy under Art 8 outweighed M's freedom of expression under Art 10. Flagrant breaches of the Press Complaints Commission's code would likely result in a violation of Art 8 rights (eg use of telephoto lens, photographs taken in private circumstances, photographs of children without consent).

Freedom of the Press v Private Life

This argument, the tension between the requirements of Articles 8 and 10, is highlighted most recently with the 'super-injunctions' argument, whereby the UK Courts installed injunctions forbidding all mention of newspaper stories involving celebrities, and even forbidding disclosure of the injunction itself. This led to the use of Parliamentary Privilege being used to name certain parties who had obtained these injunctions, and to the widespread use of Twitter being similarly utilised. This suggests that there is an increasing inability of the UK, or, perhaps, any Courts to be able to control the blogosphere adequately, and leads to the issue of whether the Convention is able to deal adequately with the problems of modern technological communication in terms of these two Articles.

There has traditionally been no recognition of a free standing right of privacy in the UK: *Kaye v Robertson* [1991], although some protection of privacy could be sought through the pre-existing tort of breach of confidence: *Argyll v Argyll* [1967]. In *A v B plc* [2002] it was suggested that public figures have to expect less privacy than anonymous individuals and the press is entitled to publish stories of interest to the public, even if the matter in question is not of public importance.

However, there is now a different line of reasoning, where in *Von Hannover v Germany* [2005], the court held that the protection of speech in public matters should be upheld only insofar as they contribute to the democratic debate. Both *Campbell v MGN* [2004] and *Murray v Express Newspaper* [2008] suggest a higher protection of privacy for public figures, but in certain circumstances only, where there could be seen to be a legitimate expectation of privacy (for instance, with children).

In *Ash v McKennitt* [2006] and *Mosley v News Group Newspaper* [2008], the UK Courts applied a stricter test of public interest, much more in line with Von Hannover. But when Moseley attempted to suggest that freedom of the press be more effectively curtailed by making them agree all stories with the parties involved, the Court in Strasbourg rejected his arguments. It considered that a general requirement of prior notification risked having a negative effect on investigative journalism, and that there should be considered a margin of appreciation for each state in terms of redress and for the protection of privacy. In the UK this includes actions for damages, injunctions and a complaints procedure through the Press Complaints Commission.

As a general rule in the UK, therefore, it seems that the criterion is that, for the information to be revealed, it must be of 'public interest' and not just of 'interest to the public'.

Article 14: Prohibition of discrimination
See *A & Others v Secretary of State for the Home Department* under Art 5 above.

Protocol 1, Art 1: Right to peaceful enjoyment of possessions
Article 1 of the First Protocol protects an individual from arbitrary interference with his or her possessions. Any law that interferes with or deprives an individual of his or her possessions will only be justified if it is in the public interest and proportionate to the aim pursued.

- *Lindsay v Commissioners of Customs and Excise* [2002]: the Court of Appeal held that the seizure and non-return of motor vehicles of those who evaded duty on tobacco and alcohol was not justified in the public interest and was not proportionate to the aim pursued. It failed to distinguish between commercial smuggling and importation for distribution among friends and family.

- *Family Housing Association v Donnellan and Others* [2002]: the rules on adverse possession in s 15 of the Limitation Act 1980 were held not to violate Protocol 1, Art 1. The court stated that the rules were a matter of private law and outside the remit of the protocol, which was directed against expropriations by the state. Furthermore, the period of 12 years gave the owner a reasonable opportunity to reassert his ownership.

Confiscation orders
- *R v Rezvi* [2002] and *R v Benjafield* [2002]: the Lords indicated that confiscation orders made under the Criminal Justice Act 1988 and the Drug Trafficking Act 1994 did not violate property rights under Protocol 1; the

provisions were a proportionate response to the problem they aimed to address, namely depriving offenders of the proceeds of their criminal conduct.

CONCLUSIONS

For an overview of the courts' approach to the HRA 1998 and the incorporation of the ECHR so far, see the table opposite.

It is clear that the HRA 1998's influence throughout the domestic legal system is immense. The raising of human rights points in court is a matter now of everyday practice. The extent to which such points have resulted in fundamental changes in the law is of course less dramatic. However, we have seen examples of the Act's dramatic influence upon the interpretation of legislation (see *R v A* above), as well as the impetus it has given to important developments in the common law (see *Douglas v Hello!* and related cases above).

In relation to the interpretation of legislation, the willingness of judges to exploit the opportunities to apply new interpretative techniques has been variable. For some commentators, progress has not been swift enough and criticism is made of judges for taking a 'minimalist' approach. *Brown v Stott* [2001] exemplified this minimalist approach when the court gave great weight to Parliament's intentions rather than to any 'Convention minded' interpretation of legislation. A similar deference to the executive was shown in *R v Secretary of State ex p Mahmood* [2001], where Laws LJ stated:

> The Human Rights Act does not authorise the judges to stand in the shoes of Parliament's delegates, who are decision-makers given their responsibilities by the democratic arm of the state. The arrogation of such a power to the judges would usurp those functions of government, which are controlled and distributed by powers whose authority is derived from the ballot-box. It follows that there must be a principled distance between the court's adjudication in a case such as this, and the Secretary of State's decision, based on his perception of the case's merits.

The courts have also taken a cautious approach in considering the retrospective application of the Act in *R v Kansal*, and also in considering where the line must

Examples of the courts' approach	
Creative interpretation of statute beyond Parliament's original intentions (*R v A*)	Deference to Parliament's original intentions in interpreting legislation (*Brown v State*; *Re W and B (Child Care Plan)* (2002))
Rigorous judicial review of administrative and executive decisions on new convention grounds (*ex p Daly*)	Deference to executive decisions, rejection of merit's based tests in judicial review (*ex p Holding and Barnes and Alconbury*)
In judicial review, Wednesbury reasonableness to be extended by tests of proportionality (*ex p Daly*)	*Wednesbury* test said to yield same result as proportionality tests (*ex p Mahmood*)
Development of new common law rights (horizontal application of HRA 1998) (*Douglas* and after)	Reliance on ECtHR jurisprudence giving large margin of appreciation to states (doctrine of due deference) (*ex p Kebilene*)

Activist ←

Minimalist →

be drawn between legitimate interpretation and the redrafting of statutes in *Re W and B (Children: Care Plan)* [2002]. There has also been an unexpectedly cautious definition of public bodies.

On the other hand, elsewhere the courts have demonstrated a much more 'activist' approach. In *R v A* [2001], which saw a radical 'reading down' of a statute to comply with the ECHR, Lord Steyn stated:

> Clearly the House [of Lords] must give weight to the decision of Parliament ... On the other hand, when the question arises whether in the criminal statute in question Parliament adopted a legislative scheme which makes an excessive inroad into the right to a fair trial, the court is qualified to make its own judgment and must do so.

This activist approach can also be seen in developments of the common law, particularly in the cases leading on from the *Douglas* case, which was said to mark 'the dawning of a substantive common law right to privacy'.

A greater willingness to develop the law was also seen in *R v Secretary of State for the Home Department ex p Daly* [2001], where Lord Steyn disapproved of the approach in *Mahmood* and emphasised the impetus that the HRA 1998 gave to new interpretative techniques of statute and to extending the common law in line with Convention rights. Lord Steyn outlined the important influence of the Act on judicial review proceedings. First, there are the new grounds for review on the basis of breach of Convention rights. Secondly, Lord Steyn confirmed the adoption of the doctrine of 'proportionality' into judicial review involving HRA 1998 claims, describing the new criteria to be applied as 'more precise and more sophisticated than the traditional grounds of review'.

The impact on judicial review is one of the most contentious debates surrounding the HRA 1998. Note that considerable 'compatibility' concerns remain among commentators regarding the principles of English public law which underlie judicial review, namely that it is a review of procedure and that it does not provide an appeal against the merits of a decision. So, while public authorities may be required to justify their actions on proportionality principles, a full review of the merits of any decision will not be undertaken by the court. Commentators suggest that these limits to judicial review will see a continuing line of cases going to Strasbourg in search of an 'effective remedy' (under ECHR, Art 13). However, in *R v Secretary of State for the Environment ex p Holding and Barnes and Others* [2001] (see above), in a judgment falling squarely into the 'minimalist' camp, the court forcefully rejected the view that judicial review was an inadequate remedy in the context of executive and administrative decisions. The court stated in that case that a full appeal on the merits would be inappropriate, in that it would subsume the Secretary of State's role in policy making in a fashion that would be undemocratic and contrary to established European jurisprudence. This appears to have put a clear stop on any hopes for the importation of merits-based criteria into judicial review, at least in respect of executive decisions. The robust view of the Law Lords was that the principles of the ECHR and the HRA 1998 make little difference to the long tradition of political and administrative decision making in the UK. However, Strasbourg has not been so unequivocal in its assessment of judicial review as an effective remedy. In *HL v UK* [2004], in the context of the detention of a mental health patient, the ECtHR reiterated its view that where intrusions upon fundamental rights are at stake, judicial review, insofar as it excludes review of the merits of a decision, is an inadequate remedy.

Clearly there are those who will argue that the long-established principles of deference to Parliament and the executive, inherent in the traditional concepts of English public law, must change in the face of modern developments in the power of the executive, but one could have anticipated that the law would not develop too radically and all at once. As Professor Helen Fenwick observes in *Civil Liberties and Human Rights* (2002): 'These dual and conflicting aspects of judicial activism and of sovereignty arise from the attempt to reconcile conflicting constitutional aims which lie at the heart of the HRA.' In any event, there will be this continuing balance between minimalist and activist approaches on the part of judges. In *International Transport Roth GmbH v Secretary of State for the Home Department* [2003] Simon Brown LJ remarked:

> Constitutional dangers exist no less in too little judicial activism as in too much. There are limits to the legitimacy of executive or legislative decision-making, just as there are to decision-making by the courts.

It is still early days for the Act, and the changes wrought by it will inevitably arrive by steady incremental growth rather than by revolution.

As Fenwick also observes, the Act provides an important opportunity to reverse the erosion of fundamental freedoms that have occurred under legislation in the last 25 years, particularly in the use of broad ranging legislation in the contexts of public protest, State surveillance and terrorist suspects' rights. So whatever the cautiousness of the judges' approach so far, the opportunity remains for the HRA 1998's ever-increasing impact on domestic law. But the effectiveness of the Act depends on three factors:

1 The willingness of judges to defend rights robustly and to challenge executive powers.
2 The willingness of governments to make remedial orders and to ensure that statements of compatibility are fully considered.
3 The vigour with which individual applicants are willing to assert their rights in a court of law.

In an article in 1996 entitled 'Does Britain need a Bill of Rights?', Ronald Dworkin lamented the loss of the culture of liberty in Britain:

Great Britain was once a fortress for freedom. It claimed the great philosophers of liberty – Milton and Locke and Paine and Mill. Its legal tradition is irradiated with liberal ideas: that people accused of crime are presumed to be innocent, that no one owns another's conscience, that a man's home is his castle, that speech is the first liberty because it is central to all the rest. But now Britain offers much less formal legal protection to central freedoms than most democracies do, including most of Britain's neighbours in Europe. These democracies have written constitutions that guarantee individual freedom, and their judges are charged with ensuring that other public officials, including legislators, respect those rights.

The HRA 1998 is a crucial step towards Britain's return to the frontiers of liberty.

You should now be confident that you would be able to tick all of the boxes on the checklist at the beginning of this chapter. To check your knowledge of Recent developments why not visit the companion website and take the Multiple Choice Question test. Check your understanding of the terms and vocabulary used in this chapter with the flashcard glossary.

6

Putting it into practice ...

Now that you've mastered the basics, you will want to put it all into practice. The Routledge Questions and Answers series provides an ideal opportunity for you to apply your understanding and knowledge of the law and to hone your essay-writing technique.

We've included one exam-style essay question, which replicates the type of question posed in the Routledge Questions and Answers series to give you some essential exam practice. The Q&A includes an answer plan and a fully worked model answer to help you recognise what examiners might look for in your answer.

QUESTION 1

Critically evaluate the current regime governing the regulation and censorship of cinema films and videos in relation to the demands of Art 10 of the European Convention on Human Rights as received into domestic law under the Human Rights Act.

Answer Plan

This is a reasonably straightforward essay question about the role of the British Board of Film Classification in regulating and censoring cinema films and videos. Bear in mind the implications flowing from the fact that the ECHR has been afforded further effect in domestic law under the HRA 1998: you need to consider the key provisions of the HRA as they relate to the regulation and censorship of films and videos; you also need to examine the relevant Strasbourg jurisprudence. The mere fact that Art 10 of the ECHR has been received into domestic law under the HRA does not necessarily mean that change is needed.

Essentially, the following areas should be considered:

- Art 10 of the ECHR and the HRA 1998;
- relevant Strasbourg jurisprudence under Art 10;
- classification and censorship of cinema films;
- the legal framework relating to films and videos;
- conclusions regarding compatibility of the regulatory regime and Art 10 of the ECHR.

AIM HIGHER

If you are able to show an appreciation of the practical context or operation of the law your answer is likely to be viewed favourably by the examiner. Sometimes the bare legal rules provide only a partial picture and you need to explore non legal matters to provide a thorough picture of the issues. See, for example, in the answer below, the discussion about the practical operation of the film classification system of regulation and the likelihood of this leading to self-censorship for commercial motives.

ANSWER

The legislation governing censorship of films and videos (the Video Recordings Act 1984 as amended and the Cinemas Act 1985) must be read by the courts in a manner which gives effect, so far as is possible, to the Convention rights (s 3 of the HRA). Further, the HRA gives particular regard to the importance of freedom of expression in s 12, although this has been interpreted by the courts as not giving Art 10 any trump status. Under s 6 of the HRA media bodies such as the British Board of Film Classification (BBFC) and the Video Appeals Committee of the BBFC (VAC) are likely to be public authorities obliged to respect Convention rights. It is argued that the independent regulation of film and video, which clearly affects the rights of those involved in production and distribution, is a function of a public nature under s 6 of the HRA. Assuming that they are public authorities, these bodies must ensure that Art 10 is not infringed in their decision making. Ultimately, decisions of media regulators or of other media bodies that are also public authorities can be challenged in the courts, which should seek to ensure that Art 10 is being complied with. Thus, it is submitted that restrictions on freedom of expression in this context may undergo fresh scrutiny, with a possible change in the balance against restraints on the showing of explicit material. Nevertheless, there have not so far been any successful challenges to decisions of the BBFC or VAC.

The regulation of films does not necessarily in itself infringe Art 10. Article 10(1) specifically provides that the Article 'shall not prevent States from requiring the licensing of broadcasting, television or cinema enterprises'. It is significant that this provision arises in the *first* paragraph of Art 10, thereby providing a limitation of the primary right that on its face is not subject to the test of para 2. However, a very restrictive approach to this sentence has been adopted. It has been found to mean that a licensing system is allowed for on grounds not restricted to those enumerated in para 2; the State may determine who is to have a licence to broadcast. But in general, other decisions of the regulatory bodies are not covered by the last sentence of para 1 and must be considered within para 2 (*Groppera Radio AG v Switzerland* [1990]). Thus, content requirements must be considered under para 2. Certain forms of expression which may be said to be of no value may fall outside the scope of Art 10(1) and it is arguable that, for example, material gratuitously offensive to religious sensibilities (*Otto-Preminger Institut v Austria* [1994], *Norwood v UK* [2005]) or depictions of genitals in pornographic magazines intended merely for entertainment (*Groppera Radio AG v Switzerland* [1990]) may fall outside its scope. On the other hand, 'hardcore' pornography has been found by the Commission to fall within Art 10(1) (*Hoare v UK* [1997]).

Political speech receives a more robust degree of protection than other types of expression. By contrast, in cases involving artistic speech, an exactly opposite pattern emerges: applicants have tended to be unsuccessful and a deferential approach to the judgments of the national authorities as to its obscene or blasphemous nature has been adopted (*Müller v Switzerland* [1991], *Handyside v UK* [1976], *Otto-Preminger Institut v Austria* [1994], *Gay News v UK* [1982]). In *Otto-Preminger Institut v Austria* [1994], the court found that a State may restrict expressions which may offend a particular population, although, otherwise, freedom of expression includes freedom to disseminate unpopular, shocking and disturbing information and ideas.

Currently, in the UK, censorship of cinema films operates in practice on two levels: first, the BBFC, a self-censoring body set up by the film industry itself in 1912, may insist on cuts before issuing a certificate allowing a film to be screened or may refuse to issue a certificate at all. Films are classified by age: 'U' films are open to anybody, as, in effect, are 'PG' (parental guidance) classified films. After that are '12'/'12A', '15' and '18' certificate films. 'R18' films (restricted viewing) may be viewed only on segregated premises. An 'R18' certificate means that the BBFC considers that the film would survive an Obscene Publications Act 1959 prosecution; it will refuse a certificate if a film is thought to fall foul of the Act. In coming to its decision, the BBFC will take the 'public good' defence under s 4(1A) of the 1959 Act, as amended, into account. This defence provides that a film or soundtrack can be justified as being for the public good 'on the ground that it is in the interests of drama, opera, ballet or any other art or of literature or learning'. Therefore, the BBFC may grant a certificate on the grounds of artistic merit to a film that contains some obscene matter. Clearly, most film distributors have no interest in achieving only a restricted publication for a film and are, therefore, prepared to make cuts to achieve a wider circulation. Thus, the system of control may be driven largely by commercial motives: a distributor may make quite stringent cuts in order to ensure that, for example, a film receives a '15' certificate and so reaches a wider audience.

The second level of censorship is operated by local authorities under the Cinemas Act 1985, which continues the old power arising under the Cinematograph Act 1909. The local authority will usually follow the BBFC's advice; authorities are reluctant to devote resources to viewing films and will tend to rely on the Board's judgment. Thus, although technically the BBFC wields no power in this area, in reality its judgments are likely to be determinative. Authorities may, on occasion, choose to grant or not to grant a licence to a film regardless of its decision. This dual system of censorship was criticised by the Williams Committee in 1979 partly on the ground of the anomalies caused by having two overlapping levels and partly due to the inconsistency between local authorities. The Video Recordings Act (VRA) 1984 was introduced after a campaign about the dangers posed by video 'nasties' to children. Under the VRA 1984, the BBFC was established as the authority charged with classifying videos for viewing in the home. Videos are classified and therefore censored in almost the same way as films, and under s 9 of the 1984 Act it is an offence to supply a video without a classification certificate, unless it is exempt on grounds of its concern with education, sport, music or religion. Under s 2(2), the exemption will not apply if the video portrays human sexual activity or gross violence or is likely to stimulate or encourage this. Further, the exemptions will not apply if a video depicts techniques likely to encourage the commission of offences.

The BBFC must have 'special regard' to harm which may be caused to 'potential viewers or through their behaviour to society' by the manner in which the film deals with criminal behaviour, illegal drugs, violent behaviour or incidents, horrific incidents or behaviour, or human sexual activity. These criteria are non-exhaustive. The kind of harm envisaged to a child or to society is not specified and nor is the degree of seriousness envisaged. There is a right of appeal from the decisions of the BBFC to the VAC, under s 4, which operates as a tribunal.

The stance of the BBFC is obviously influenced by the composition of the Board, but its effect on film and video makers has been criticised as militating against creativity. It has been suggested by Robertson that a cosy relationship has developed that is insufficiently challenging – the acceptable boundaries are not fully explored in the name of artistic integrity and creative freedom. The age-based classification system encourages commercial judgments rather than artistic considerations to dominate; the most pressing consideration is to find the widest audience, which may mean instituting cuts in order to obtain a '15' certificate. These factors lead to a heavier censorship of films in the UK than in Europe or the US.

It seems possible that the inception of the HRA could have some impact on this situation. For example, a film maker whose film was refused a classification without certain cuts could seek to challenge the decision of the BBFC or, in the case of a video, that of the VAC, upholding the BBFC's decision. The VAC and BBFC are, assuming that they are public authorities, bound by the Convention rights under s 6 of the HRA. Therefore, they should ensure that their decisions do not breach Art 10 or any other relevant Article. One potential problem for aggrieved film makers is that the courts are likely to defer to a significant extent to the specialist regulatory bodies as has been the case with press regulation: *R (Ford) v Press Complaints Commission* [2001].

The 1984 Act, as amended, must be interpreted compatibly with the Convention rights. Given that a number of its terms are very open-ended, there is room for a range of interpretations. In actions against the BBFC, the court would have to give effect to s 12 of the HRA. Although this requires particular regard to be given to the importance of Art 10 this has been interpreted in cases such as *Campbell v MGN* [2004] to include not just the right but also the restrictions in Art 10(2). Thus it affords no special status to freedom of expression.

The stance taken by Strasbourg in relation to films likely to offend religious sensibilities was indicated in the leading decision, *Otto-Preminger* [1994]. The film in question was not likely to be viewed by children, but was found to be offensive to religious sensibilities. The seizure and forfeiture of the film was not found to breach Art 10. Further guidance derives from the decision of the Court of Human Rights in *Wingrove v UK* [1996]. This judgment concerned a decision of the BBFC, upheld by the VAC, to refuse a certificate to the short, explicit film *Visions of Ecstasy*. The Court found that the decision to refuse a certificate was within the national authorities' margin of appreciation. The film, which was to be promulgated as a short video, was viewed as offensive to religious sensibilities and as quite likely to come to the attention of children, since it could be viewed in the home. No breach of Art 10 was found.

In the case of a sexually explicit or violent film, the problem would be, as indicated above, that the Strasbourg jurisprudence appears to support quite far-reaching restrictions. However, where the risk of children viewing the film is very slight due to the use of age restrictions relating to films to be shown in the cinema, *and* the question of offending religious sensibilities does not arise, it is suggested that the jurisprudence can be viewed as supporting the availability of even very explicit films. This contention derives from the principles underlying the jurisprudence, which, as indicated above, relate to the familiar free speech justifications, including that of self-fulfilment.

It is concluded that where the question of offence to religious sensibilities does not arise it would be consonant with the general Strasbourg freedom of expression jurisprudence to leave little scope under Art 10(2) for interferences with the freedom of expression of film makers in respect of films targeted at adults. Different considerations would apply to videos, owing to the possibility that they might be viewed by children, although this argument should be considered carefully in terms of its impact on adults. The question of the harm that might be caused should also be considered, bearing in mind the lack of evidence regarding a connection between behaviour seen on film and actual behaviour. The mere invocation of the possibility that children might view a video should not be enough. Guidance on this matter might usefully be sought from other jurisdictions, since it is not a matter that Strasbourg has inquired into in any depth.

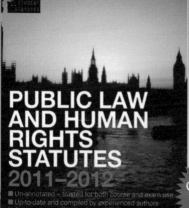